ALSO BY AUDREY RICKER AND CAROLYN CROWDER

Backtalk: 4 Steps to Ending Rude Behavior in Your Kids

Whining

3 Steps
to Stopping It
Before the
Tears
and Tantrums
Start

AUDREY RICKER, Ph.D.
CAROLYN CROWDER, Ph.D.

A Fireside Book
Published by Simon & Schuster
New York   London   Sydney   Singapore

FIRESIDE
Rockefeller Center
1230 Avenue of the Americas
New York, NY 10020

FIRESIDE and colophon are registered trademarks
of Simon & Schuster Inc.

Designed by Elina Nudelman

Manufactured in the United States of America

1   3   5   7   9   10   8   6   4   2

Library of Congress Cataloging-in-Publication Data is available.

ISBN 0-684-85742-1

ACKNOWLEDGMENTS

We would like to thank our agent, Alice Martell, for her consistent hard work on our behalf and our editor, Becky Cabaza at Simon & Schuster, for her patience and innate understanding of the principles we are trying to teach herein. Also, our thanks to Sue Fleming for her ongoing dedication to promoting our books.

Audrey Ricker would also like to thank media theorist Eileen Meehan, and educator Robert Calmes, for their willingness to share knowledge and ideas with her when she was writing her part of this book.

We credit the Adlerian psychology community with the ongoing development of Adler's and Dreikurs' ideas and the larger counseling profession for insights into the use and benefits of assertiveness theory and techniques.

Many of the more delightful and provocative turns of phrase used in this book come from the teachings of Oscar Christensen. He has given his professional life to the betterment of our society by training counselors, teachers, psychologists, and parents in ways to treat children respectfully.

To Marcia Amsterdam and Janis de Vries. Also, I dedicate this book to professional researcher Elizabeth Felicetti and to my family members Joshua, Antonia, Sophia, and Isabella Ricker.

A.R.

To my dad.

C.C.

CONTENTS

INTRODUCTION

• •

Pam walks in the house having just picked up her two children at school. On the drive home, she had told both children that she had to make some work-related phone calls as soon as they got home. She asked the children to take their school things to their rooms and change clothes while she conducted her business.

Once at home, however, the children dump their school bags on the living room floor and fly into the kitchen whining that they're hungry, they need snacks, they must have some milk and cookies right away.

Pam reminds them that she's asked for a few minutes to make some business calls, and she asks them once again to put their things away and change clothes.

At this point, the children begin to whine loudly, bickering with each other as they stand before the open refrigerator door, taking matters into their own hands. Pam is now at a loss. She's promised to make some calls for her fledgling real estate business, and she's already late. She wishes her children would cooperate and give her the few minutes she needs. She begs them to just let her make a couple of calls. They turn teary faces to her as they beg back for cookies.

She wonders if she's asking too much of a six-

and an eight-year-old. Their pleading stirs her guilt. When Bobby pulls the milk out of the refrigerator and spills it all over the kitchen floor, she loses her temper, yelling at them to get away from her and go to their rooms.

Spilled milk? Yelling? Whining? Guilt? Parental self-doubt? Pam and her children have experienced all these things and more in their brief trip to the "whine cellar." Do you have a "whine cellar" in your home? Are your kids in it a lot? Do you find yourself going down there on occasion?

If you're like Pam the only things you can think of to do when your children whine are to whine back at them or become angry. Yet, in your heart you know there have to be better ways of responding. This book is about those better ways.

Few things can reduce parents to jelly or make them feel more like failures than the spectacle created by their children's misbehavior, whether it occurs in public or at home. It is difficult enough when children act out within the family unit, but raised eyebrows and critical looks from strangers witnessing "bad" behavior from our children magnify our inadequacies and make us feel as if we're not up to the challenge of child rearing.

Yet every child at times will test our limits, jockeying for power and trying to get the upper hand. A key weapon children use is whining—the loud, pitiful, grating, or whimpering sounds that every parent has experienced. And while every parent knows the nightmare of whining children, very few have even a clue about how to deal with it.

Consider the following incidents:

- Parents are driving an unfamiliar route to attend a meeting for which they are already late. In the backseat, three-year-old Gina and four-year-old Nick have grown bored. They see a McDonald's with a shiny new playground up front. Both children begin to whine loudly, demanding that Dad stop. When he doesn't, they begin hitting each other and yelling, creating a situation that is not just distressing but also dangerous as parental tempers flare (and Dad tries to control the car).
- Lindsey needs new shoes and accompanies her mother to the mall to make the purchase. Inside the store, eleven-year-old Lindsey spies some terribly overpriced sneakers with the logo that all the kids at school are wearing. Mom says no and asks Lindsey to make another selection. Lindsey begs, pleads, and loudly whines as other customers and salesclerks look on.
- Daniel's parents have repeatedly told him not to leave his skateboard outside the house at night. One night the eight-year-old forgets to bring the board inside, and the next morning he wakes to find it has been stolen. Daniel runs whining to Mom. His world has ended. His beloved skateboard is gone: she must replace it.
- Twelve-year-old Melody is out of school for summer vacation. She wants to meet her friends after dark at the local skating rink. When her mother says she is too busy to drive her, not to mention the late hour, Melody insists she can walk. Mother says no, and Melody begins to whine and plead, using the old "all the other kids get to do it" routine. She accuses her

mother of not trusting her, and retreats to her bedroom in tears, slamming doors along the way.

- At a holiday gathering at Grandmother's house, fifteen-year-old Matthew is watching television with his adult relatives. His dad comes in the room and asks Matthew to go outside and keep an eye on his younger brother, who is in the swimming pool, while Dad goes to the store to pick up the charcoal he forgot to bring. Matt begins to whine and complain that he wants to watch the program and shouldn't have to babysit. He sulks and turns away, muttering that he's not the parent anyway, and does not move.

Parents know all too well that what begins as whining can quickly escalate into a full-blown tantrum, and most parents will avoid that ugly conflict at all costs. If the incident occurs in public and parents do nothing in response, the opportunity for teaching children how to behave is long gone by the time the parents get the children home and out of the public eye.

Whining may become a staple of the children's daily lives, something they use to get their way in the privacy of the home just as effectively as in public.

Here's an example of a lost opportunity when a parent forgoes teaching his children respectful behavior and gives in because that is easier:

••

Dan, father of three boys, agrees to take them to the video store to rent a movie for Saturday night. He tells them as they leave the house that they can rent only one movie, since on other weekends the family has wasted money by rent-

ing three and never watching them. The boys agree and off they all go.

Once in the store, the brothers begin to squabble over which movie to rent, which, of course, leads them to begin whining to their father. One boy accuses the other of always getting his way; another complains that renting just one video is not fair.

Dan threatens to take them home if they can't agree on which movie to rent. They shrug him off, knowing his threat is empty, and continue to argue among themselves.

People in the store can't help but notice the boys' rude behavior and shoot accusing looks at Dan as if he is failing to act properly in his role as a parent. After several minutes of continued whining by the children and scathing looks from the other customers, Dan throws up his hands and yells at his sons to "just go get what you want and let's get out of here."

The sons, having gotten their way, high-five each other and race down the aisles to select their videos. Dan stands alone, feeling defeated and weak, as if his own children have beaten him at some game that he wasn't even aware they were playing.

••

Dan has just missed a golden opportunity to teach his children how to behave in public. Instead, he trained them how to use whining, arguing, fighting, and complaining to get their way. You can bet that this scenario will occur again and again, because the boys know it works.

Like many parents who find themselves in this situation, Dan backed down by appeasing his sons to keep the peace and restore some quiet, but the three boys have learned nothing about working with each other, cooperating with Dad, or showing respect for others—including the other people in the video store.

Many parents like Dan feel helpless, especially in a public situation where their children's whining is drawing the attention of others. They feel there is nothing they can do *but* appease when faced with their children's misbehavior. However, parents must remember that whining is just a first step that can escalate to backtalk, arguing, and tantrums. Trying to appease whining children is a losing proposition. You're not going make them happy by giving in; they'll simply whine more. If you think the whining causes critical stares, just wait until the escalating tantrum occurs because you've failed to give them what they want.

Whining can be stopped. You can stop it by the way you respond to your child. In our first book, *Backtalk: 4 Steps to Ending Rude Behavior in Your Kids*, we taught you practical techniques for handling your children's

Remember:
When your child whines, look at it as a golden opportunity for intervention, but only if you respond in a way that teaches the child how to behave. If yelling, threatening, giving in, or punishing worked to stop your child's whining, you wouldn't need this book. Be honest with yourself and you'll realize that there has to be a better way.

rude verbal behaviors. In this book we give you three ways of responding to whining that work and that are built on respect for yourself as well as for the child.

Consequences

In this method, your child's whining is met with consequences that occur as a result of the child's misbehavior. For example, when your child whines in public, you immediately take the child home without comment. The logical consequence for not behaving in a public place is that they don't get to be there.

Consequences are most effective if they are logical and immediate. The earlier you begin using logical consequences, the fewer problems you'll have with your children later on. Using consequences works with even the youngest child. In fact, some people find this most effective with very young children who have not yet established patterns of misbehavior.

Most parents talk too much. Instead of taking action, they fuss, lecture, and threaten; meanwhile, the whining continues. Establishing consequences requires very few words, and these should be respectful, clear, and neutral in tone.

Assertiveness

This method encourages the substitution of calm, respectful dialogue that gives a child a mode of communication to *replace whining*. Children learn to ask for what they want and to articulate their desires without tantrums or manipulation. Parents must model assertiveness for their children and establish it as the typical mode of communication within the family. (Note: This is different from the "assertiveness" you've experienced in business or social situations.)

When you talk to your children, whether it be setting up consequences, following through, or stating how you feel about something, you must always be assertive (take the leadership role), respectful, and calm. We're going to give examples of this type of respectful language as well as provide you with an Assertive Communication Formula that you can use to address whining and other serious issues *after you've dealt with misbehavior by establishing consequences.*

The Assertive Communication Formula is especially effective when parents need to talk about value-based issues with their children. We urge you to use this method sparingly (the less you use it, the more impact it will have) to let your children know how you feel about very important topics like lying, stealing, physical or verbal abuse, or other behaviors that may result if whining works for children and they escalate into these other areas.

Contribution

The underlying principle of contribution is simple but effective. Contribution means that children are expected to work for the common good just as adult members of the family do. When children are made to feel they are important to the family by contributing and belonging in positive ways, they have no need to use negative behaviors such as whining to gain that feeling of importance.

These three methods work independently or together depending upon the situation. For example, consequences should be used routinely in response to whining. Any talking done around the setting up of consequences should be minimal and respectful in tone—in other words, assertive. When the whining escalates into more serious misbehaviors that challenge the parents' values, we recommend adding the formula for assertiveness as well. Contribution combats all misbehavior and should be an expectation of every member of the family, including the very youngest.

Children who contribute have a positive sense of belonging, and empathy for others soon replaces the need to act out. From the youngest to the oldest, contribution allows everyone to feel important by working for the good of the family as a whole.

For those of you wondering why in the world children would want to provoke negative reactions in adults, we provide a model to help you understand the purpose of misbehavior and why changing your response works to stop whining. This model is rooted in the theories of two pioneering psychiatrists: Alfred Adler and Rudolph Dreikurs. The ideas we present are based on their techniques, which were developed from 1900 through the 1960s.

The commonsense approach that we provide here is, therefore, nothing new, but it is very much needed in these days of indulgent parenting when adults flip-flop between giving in and making idle threats to punish. Our three methods can be used with a child of any age—and, dare we suggest it, any adult—who whines.

Even very young children who do not yet understand words and sentences will understand tone, body language, and consistency. While these methods work with all age groups, the earlier you begin the easier your parenting job will be.

What we prescribe here is simple but not easy, because it requires you to think before you act or speak and requires you to have a plan of discipline that you follow consistently each time a whining incident occurs. The chapters cover the following topics:

- Definition of whining
- Negative effects of whining upon children
- The purpose of whining
- How parents mishandle situations
- Methods for stopping whining
- Teaching your child to make requests respectfully
- The importance of contribution by children as an antidote to misbehavior

We also provide a workbook with exercises you can use to teach yourself and your children new modes of communicating. We include a fourteen-day diary that you can use to chart your progress in responding to your children's whining and misbehavior. By taking careful notes you'll begin to analyze patterns of negative behavior in yourself and in your children. More important, by keeping a record of the changes you are making in your own responses, you'll begin to recognize improvements in your family's relationships.

HOW WE WOULD LIKE YOU TO READ THIS BOOK

First, we suggest that you read this book in one or two sittings so that you get a feel for the methods we suggest. Some of the ideas we're presenting will be new to you, and you'll need to think about how to go about making the changes we're suggesting.

You need not grasp every detail; just read for an overview of the problems and their solutions, and think of ways you can begin to try some of these approaches. It does help to think about the instances of whining you experience with your children and identify specific

Remember:
- Consequences teach that whining doesn't work.
- Assertiveness teaches your child to communicate respectfully.
- Contribution teaches empathy and responsibility.

areas that are going to need the most work. The more thinking you do, the more easily you'll be able to plan and implement positive changes within your family.

Finally, once you've embarked upon your quest to rid your life of incessant whining, go back and read the chapters you feel are most helpful to you. This is *your* book. *Write in the margins!* Use the workbook and begin tracking your progress as you work toward eliminating whining behavior once and for all.

CHAPTER ONE

The Definition of Whining

When adults are asked to define whining the answers usually sound like this:

"The begging that drives me crazy . . ."

"Crying and whimpering that makes me feel sorry for them . . ."

"Once it starts, I know it's not going to stop until I give in . . ."

What these parents are doing is describing what whining is like *for them.* They know that it upsets their equilibrium and that they feel manipulated. What parents need to understand is that *whining is a technique* children use to get their way. It is as simple as that— and it *is* manipulative. Adults feel embarrassed, like Dan in the opening example, and defeated—and often get very angry and resentful, especially when the children whine in public.

Here are examples of how children whine:

- Nagging or irritating tone of voice
- Self-pitying words and phrases designed to make parents feel inadequate ("Everybody else has these shoes, why can't I? I'll look funny. Kids will laugh at me.")
- Contorted or sad facial expressions, tears, and sniffling
- Body language (slumped shoulders, heads down, pleading hand gestures)
- Loud, incessant demands (especially in public where the child knows that others are watching and parents are likely to give in, to avoid a scene)

HOW WHINING GETS STARTED

Children are not born knowing how to whine. But they usually hit upon it at an early age. They hear older brothers and sisters, children on television, or friends at preschool whining—and sometimes they even hear it from Mom and Dad.

Among adults, whining usually takes the guise of complaints like "Look at all I've done for you, and I'm just asking you to do this one little thing for me . . ." Children try it themselves and quickly find out that whining works—especially if they keep it up for a long enough time. They know parents will wear down and cave in!

••

Andrea is the mother of Katie, age three, and Kurt, age six. While Kurt is busily involved in school and soccer, little Katie is involved in whining just about all the time. Whenever her mother leaves the room or tries to put her down, Katie begins to whimper and complain.

"I don't want you to think I don't play with my daughter, but I can't even get a load of laundry out of the dryer without Katie whining. It makes me feel awful." Andrea sighs. "My pediatrician says she is having separation anxiety and will outgrow it in time, but I just can't stand the whining."

Andrea and her husband are particularly disappointed because they spent much of last summer doing special things with Katie in an attempt to lighten her moods and make her cheerful. They went to the beach and zoo and played lots of games, but Katie whined her way through it all. She was unable to enjoy anything unless Andrea was right there with her, giving her 100 percent of her attention. "I couldn't even speak to anyone else without Katie whimpering," Andrea confides.

Andrea thinks that she must have neglected Katie in her infancy somehow, and that is what has made this child so dependent. "Maybe I spent too much time with Kurt and she was hurt by that," she muses. Andrea also wonders if the truth is just that she is a failure at mothering two children.

She notes that her neighbor has three children, including a daughter who is Katie's age and who rarely whines. Andrea wonders what people think. "I'll be having this great conversation with my neighbor in the backyard and it starts. Katie wants me to pick her up. I feel ashamed for having such a needy child."

Andrea also feels resentment. "I do so much for Katie. I cater to her most of the time. I can't

**even get away for a movie once in a while, be-
cause she goes into a total meltdown when I try
to walk out the door."**

THE NEGATIVE EFFECTS OF WHINING ON PARENTS AND CHILDREN

Katie whines to get her way. She has adopted what
we refer to as a "mistaken" way of belonging. Children,
like all of us, need to feel that they have a place of significance in the home—and will find that place through
either constructive or destructive means.

Whining makes Katie feel important and powerful,
and she has learned to belong in this family by being
the whimpering, dependent child, forever the "baby" of
the family. Our chapter on contribution will explain
how important it is that your children be encouraged to
find a place through behaviors such as helping, assuming responsibilities, and thinking of others.

For right now, suffice it to say that Katie rules the
roost with her "weakness." Whining works for her in that
she gets what she wants and feels powerful. It is quite
heady for a child to be able to elicit exasperation, anger,
retaliation and, finally, giving in from a grown-up.

Katie will continue to whine and control in her bid for
power and attention as long as her parents reinforce
her behavior with the wrong responses.

For Katie, the ability to provoke her parents is a sign
of her power. She finds a place in the family by control-
ling others. Katie knows at some level that her mother
has doubts about what to do, and she exploits her
mother's lack of confidence by appearing weak and dependent.

When Andrea gives in, she's responding not just to

Wrong Responses to Whining:
- giving in to the child's demands
- exhibiting irritation
- showing anger or resentment
- engaging in retaliation

Katie's "tyranny of weakness" but also to her own self-doubts about her ability as a parent. Don't get us wrong—we are not saying that Katie is deliberately *thinking about* and using these misbehaviors for the purpose of feeling powerful and important. She has merely hit upon these behaviors that bring her these powerful feelings, and so she repeats them as long as they work. That is why parental response is so important.

If allowed to continue, Katie's "mistaken" way of belonging can follow her into adulthood, becoming part of her basic approach to life. Manipulation of others through whining and a need to be the center of attention may hinder her success in all areas of life and will harm her chances to create mature, lasting relationships.

She may spend a lifetime feeling victimized by others because she never learned to be independent and forthright. Worse yet, she never learned to have empathy for others.

OTHER DANGERS OF WHINING

Whining isn't something that goes away on its own. You do your child a great disservice when you think of whining as "only a stage" the child is going through.

The effects of whining may be long-term and destructive to every member of the family. Here's why:

- Whining is contagious! When one child in the family starts, and it works, the others will try it, too. Older sister wants a snack, but Mother says no because dinner's almost ready. The younger siblings take up the cry: "We're hungry, too . . . why can't we eat . . . give me a cookie . . . I don't want to wait . . . I'm so hungry right now."

- Whining can lead to self-pity, seriously immobilizing the child when trying new things. "I don't want to play soccer . . . I'm no good . . . I can't do it . . . you're mean to make me."

- Whining can lead to the belief that the child is a "loser," because parents may buy into the youngster's "neediness" and dependency, seeing the child as "less" than other children. This self-fulfilling prophecy can foster weakness and vulnerability in the child's own self-perception. "Bobby's not like other children . . . he gets his feelings hurt . . . I have to protect him from other children . . . that game's too rough . . . he'll get hurt." Worse yet, the child may harbor deep resentment toward the parents because of these low opinions they express about the child's abilities.

- Whining doesn't get better. If ignored, it just turns into rebellion and even more destructive behavior. "You told me I could go . . . now you're saying I can't . . . I'm going anyway . . . I don't care what you say."

- Whining can make children unpopular with peers and teachers and, if left unchecked, can become a problem with spouses, bosses, and friends in adulthood. "You never listen to me . . . I need for you to understand me . . . I need more time . . . I can't do it the way you want me to . . . You have to do it for me . . . It's too hard."

- Whining can escalate into a full-blown temper tantrum. "I want to watch *Barney* . . . let me watch it now. I hate you . . . I hate you . . . Daddy lets me watch *Barney.*" The whining has become screaming by now, and many times children will break something, throw toys, or hold their breath while they kick and roll around on the floor.

While it is true that some children may outgrow whining as they get older, this is the exception, not the rule. Misbehavior doesn't usually correct itself without parental intervention. Children who give up whining on their own usually do so because they've found more efficient, but usually not more constructive, ways of getting their needs met. These children may turn to dangerous behaviors like lying, stealing, or sneaking out after hours. Their bids for attention (which they no longer get from whining) can even involve self-destructive behaviors like drug and alcohol abuse.

Sometimes children give up whining because they are made fun of once too often by other kids who love to

Remember:
 Adults should never mimic children. Ridicule only sets up a cycle of retaliation between you and your children.

mimic them. But don't think this technique works for parents. When you make fun of your child as a means of discipline, you cause hurt and teach your child that it is okay to hurt others and to use revenge as a weapon.

TYPES OF WHINING

Whining takes many forms. See if you recognize any of these:

The Detail-Oriented Whine

"Mommy, you said you'd play two games of Go Fish and one game of pick-up sticks and read *The Little Mermaid* twice if I was good while you were on the phone. I was good, wasn't I?"

The child recites promises made by her mother to get her to behave while Mom was on the phone. The parent made a serious mistake in trying to manipulate her daughter into good behavior, and now she faces the daunting task of following through on her promises. Her daughter is already whining and gearing up for a fight.

The Negotiation Whine

"I promise you I'll do all my homework Sunday night if you'll just buy me that new computer game I want." After you've already said no to the computer game, the child tries to wear you down by negotiating, with promises of good behavior in return for what he wants. The whining is escalating, even though it may appear that the child is offering a reasonable solution.

The Desperation Whine

"Please buy me this outfit for the school party. I have to have it or else all the kids will think I'm weird. I can't possibly wear the one you already bought!" The child conveys frantic worry and leans on the parents to rescue her. The implication is that a "good" parent will provide what the child so desperately needs in order to be part of the peer group and stave off the humiliation of being different. It is only "bad" parents who don't care enough about their child to rush out and buy what the child wants when the child is suffering.

The Self-Pitying Whine

"I can't go out for soccer because I can't do it. I'm just no good at it." The parents feel helpless and sorry for their child. Their hearts break as they wonder what to say and do in response. If parents agree with the child, they're admitting the child is deficient. If they disagree, they worry that they may be putting the child in a situation that will result in failure. It is the proverbial "rock and a hard place." When parents don't know which way to go, they give in, allowing the child to dictate what will happen next.

The Theatrical Whine

Almost all whining has a touch of drama. "I have to go to Aunt Joan's this weekend to get that sweater I left over there. Jessica wants to borrow it and she'll never be my friend again if I don't get it to her!" Such whining can quickly proceed to backtalk like "You have to take me now. I need this and you never do anything that's important to me." Parents usually succumb to this type of manipulation just so the child will be quiet.

Bear in mind that the above examples are typical of the types of whining that older, more verbal children engage in. Very young children who cannot yet use language have their own system of whimpering, sniffling, and crying to attempt to get their way. It is all whining, and parents should have a plan about how to respond to it.

GIVING IN TO WHINING DOESN'T WORK

Many people might say that Katie's behavior in the earlier example should be given in to, because it is a true cry for more quality time with Andrea. Working moms like Andrea may believe their busy schedules and time away from their children necessitate giving in to whining.

But you notice that when Andrea gives Katie what she wants, the problem doesn't disappear. In fact, the whining seems to increase. "The more time I spend with Katie, the more dependent she becomes and the less self-sufficient. I don't know what else to do, because her whining and whimpering gets me every time. I feel so bad for her."

The problem here is not that Andrea gives her daughter too little time or is a bad mother. The problem is that she gets hooked into guilt feelings (her vulnerable spot) and cannot figure out how to free herself. While she knows better intellectually, Andrea reacts to every whine as a legitimate cry for help that she as a mother must not ignore.

Giving in to whining keeps it going, because children learn that if they continue long enough and loud enough, parents will eventually succumb to the pressure. Therefore we adults need to respond very differently. We often give in after we have yelled, lectured, or ridiculed and thereby think we have "disciplined" them. As children become more adept at whining, they refine their skills, increasing their chances of being successful in manipulating to get what they want.

•••

Olivia, thirteen, states that she argues with almost everything her parents say, as do many of her friends. "When Mom tells me that I can't go out until I do my math—I hate doing it—I usually say, 'Mother, you know I do math better when I wake up in the morning and have my Diet Coke.'

"She says, 'How many times do I have to tell you no soda in the morning?' and we're off and running. The math, the Diet Coke, going out with my friends for a pizza or whatever, it doesn't matter.

"I argue and whine and whine and argue until Mom is so cross-eyed that she can't remember which argument to stick to most and so she says, 'Just go, and no more Diet Cokes in the morning.' If I'm tired of the arguing and whining, I say, 'Okay, I promise' and then just do it anyway."

•••

The argument whine is a disrespectful way for an older child to try to assert independence, and indulging it is bad for the child. This cycle of disrespectful behavior—whining and arguing, and the eventual giving in—wears everyone out and keeps the household in turmoil.

Olivia's mother states, "It's like I'm living in a bad movie. Nothing really happens and nobody ever has a good time." What is described here is pretty much anarchy. Mom has provided no structure to deal with Olivia's misbehavior.

WHAT CHILDREN WHINE ABOUT MOST

Most parents have the same problems with their kids. Nearly every child tries whining at some point, and here are the most common areas that kids whine about:

Television and computer limits
Bedtime
Waking up
Getting dressed
Eating
Homework
Sharing with siblings
Wanting or not wanting to go to certain places
Babysitters
Where to sit in the car
Chores

This isn't a complete list, but we're sure that many of you have experienced problems that involve all these arenas of family interaction. How did we get to the point where whining is so common?

PUTTING WHINING IN PERSPECTIVE

When people think of the "good old days in parenting," they are often referring to autocratic methods of discipline that used to work in a culture where the belief was that "children should be seen and not heard." The irony here is that most of us were raised that way and don't want our children to experience the same ironhanded parental authority model in which children did as they were told because they feared their parents.

In this "golden age" of parenting, adults ruled the roost (usually Dad was in first place) and meted out spankings, lectures, humiliation, and retribution to make sure that children behaved.

With the advent of a more permissive, free society in the 1960s, many parents used the exact opposite of the old autocratic methods and became more and more indulgent with their children. At the same time, children began asserting their rights, concluding that they should not tolerate hitting and yelling from adults. We are now witnessing the phenomenon of children going to court to "divorce" their parents, often because of physical or verbal abuse they've suffered.

Several other changes have influenced the parent/child relationship since that time. All forms of media are readily available. Children are targeted by manufacturers and advertisers and are pulled toward certain products, which then play a major role in the whining game.

- School-age girls may feel that they must have the right hair, clothes, and body to be accepted by others.
- Preschoolers may want to have the same cereal the cartoon characters are selling on television.
- Most children want the latest series of books, CDs, backpacks and collectible figures spawned by big-budget children's movies and the barrage of licensed media products that go along with them.
- Older boys often want to play video games for hours on end.
- Adolescents want shoes, exercise clothing, and other equipment advertised by well-known sports figures or celebrities.
- Children of all ages may not want to give up their earphones for any reason.

Children may be convinced they must have certain products in order to be like everybody else, and they'll whine endlessly until their parents succumb to the pressure to buy them. Today's children also watch more television, see more films, and are exposed to more forms of popular culture where bad behavior may be modeled. All of these things can contribute to problems between parent and child. (In fact, the American Academy of Pediatricians recently recommended that parents remove televisions and personal computers from children's bedrooms, and that no children under the age of two be exposed to television.)

How should parents react when they are told, often by experts, that the constant barrage of advertising and media *causes* whining and misbehavior in their children? Some experts claim that studies show that aggression is linked to violent movies and television. But it is very difficult to prove causality for any kind of behavior. That is why we prefer to look for the purpose of the behavior—what does whining bring to children?

While media hype can make it more difficult for parents to teach and discipline their children, parents are still the most powerful influences for their children, even through the teen years. The best response you can have to these potentially negative influences is a strong, mutually respectful relationship with your child. Children need a firm foundation in life, and it must come through your parenting.

It is much more respectful for parents to convey to their children that when they whine, they are making a decision to do so. It does none of us any good to make excuses for our own or our children's behavior. They are not merely little victims of the "bad" culture, and such a belief is disrespectful in its premise. They are whining

> *Remember:*
> The most important influence upon children is not the media but the actions of parents who clarify for their children what is really important and what values they want the family to subscribe to.

because the technique has worked with their parents in the past, not because the children have seen examples of whining on television and are compelled to mimic the behavior.

"Monkey see, monkey do" is no excuse for whining or any other negative behavior. To adopt the attitude that children are only mimicking actions they see on television, as opposed to making choices of their own, lets both children and parents off the hook. In neither case is there an emphasis on taking responsibility for actions and making a concerted effort to do things differently.

How do you as a parent respond to the media? Do you indulge in a buying frenzy when you watch advertising on television? If you do, then your children will, too. Do you know what your children are watching and listening to? Part of your parental role is to interpret popular culture and take a stand as needed so that your children will be able to do the same.

Well-raised children are less vulnerable to media hype or peer pressure, because their parents have schooled them to resist being manipulated by advertising and to feel good about themselves without succumbing to a materialistic lifestyle. These children have a strong sense of who they are and how they belong without having to have a particular stuffed animal or a logo-bearing pair of shoes. Sometimes it seems that parents buy all this stuff as a substitute for spending time with their children. Good parenting takes a large investment of time.

Many parents have indulged children to the point of creating such tyrants that no one wants to be around them. These parents do not trust their own common sense when it comes to raising their children. They give in constantly to their children's demands, rationalize their bad behaviors away, and generally indulge and appease in order to have "peace" in the family. The sad thing is that indulging children doesn't achieve harmony for long. Very soon the bad behavior begins again. It works too well for the children to just give it up on their own.

Many parents are afraid to assume the leadership role of setting limits and educating their children—or they simply don't know how because they were not taught these things when young themselves. It is easy to fall back on the behaviors we remember our parents using when we were small. Change is difficult, and sometimes adults are just too tired to argue or too preoccupied with other concerns to provide the time it takes to discipline a child in a respectful way.

Most parenting reactions are just that—reactive—with no general plan based on knowing how children need to be treated in order to grow into responsible adults.

CHAPTER TWO

The Purpose of Whining

Children don't whine just to hear themselves make noise. They always have an agenda. Consider the following case:

• •

Sandy is the mother of four-year-old Joey. She finds her son hard to resist and indulges him most of the time. This particular day, Grandmother was visiting and both grownups were at their wits' end about how to satisfy and humor Joey.

He had begun whining soon after Grammy's arrival and had not stopped. First he was not happy at breakfast because his favorite cereal was all gone and he wanted nothing else. Grandmother solved this problem by dashing off to the store to buy more. After a few bites, he put down his spoon and began whining that he didn't want this cereal after all.

They offered to fix him toast and eggs, but he continued to whine that he wanted none of these things. Sandy and her mother agreed that he must not be feeling well, and that would explain his "bad mood."

When it was time for preschool, Joey cried that he didn't want to go, and Grammy concluded that he wanted to stay home with her . . . so stay home he did.

These two women spent the rest of the day trying to cheer Joey up, and nothing they did—even going to the mall to buy a toy he had been wanting or eating at his favorite fast-food restaurant—got him to stop whimpering and whining. But because he never escalated into a full-blown tantrum, Sandy and her mother felt it had been a pretty good day!

WHAT JOEY REALLY WANTED

Like most parents, Sandy believed that Joey's requests and demands were legitimate. A child needs to eat breakfast. A "good" parent provides food. If the child will eat only one kind of cereal, a "good" parent must provide that kind of cereal. You handle one demand and move on to the next.

The fact that the time together is tense and centered almost exclusively on the child is not noticed, nor is the fact that the child is being taught to be demanding, picky, and uncaring about what others may want or need.

For Mom, the issue is breakfast. But for Joey, breakfast cereal is what he uses to gain attention or demonstrate his power and thereby reinforce his "mistaken" sense of belonging. If Grammy runs to the store to do as he wishes, then he feels important.

Mom and Grammy are failing to teach Joey to think about his behavior in terms of how it affects others. Joey only wants to get his way. Breakfast, preschool, toys, and eating are the arenas in which he plays out his desire for attention and power. The sense of control over others is the real purpose behind his whining.

In order to learn to think of others, children must learn to have empathy and develop the ability for give-and-take in relationships. Children don't whine because they are "bad." Rather, they have hit upon whining as something that works to make them feel powerful and to get what they want.

These children haven't learned that empathy for others and a cooperative spirit provide them a way of belonging that is much more harmonious and satisfying. Parents who indulge whining are cheating their children out of the opportunity to find a positive place within the family.

A child like Joey has not learned that there are other ways of feeling important in the family because he has been pampered and catered to since birth. A mistake many parents make is thinking that children cannot be expected to contribute to the household because they are too young or because they don't know how. It is a disservice to think that any child is too young to learn to help or to think of the needs and rights of others in his family.

Each child needs to be part of the maintenance and running of the household—all of those responsibilities (laundry, meals, vacuuming, trash) that are usually carried by Mother or Dad can be done in whole or in part by even the youngest child.

When we prevent a toddler from helping us take out the trash or wash the dishes, we're denying that child a contributing role in the family. What's worse, we're setting up a situation that can lead the child to try to gain attention and power in negative ways such as whining.

In defense of parents, most come home tired, frustrated, and tense, not the best state for encouraging their children to do tasks around the house. It is easier to place a toddler in front of the television while Mom and Dad get dinner ready. However, what parents don't realize is that by using their own states of exhaustion or frustration to put off educating their children, they're creating greater problems.

A toddler may not do a task perfectly, but a parent is better off allowing the child to contribute than depriving the child of this opportunity.

Empathy and cooperation cannot flourish if parents move their children aside and don't allow them to learn to belong in positive ways. The goal of parents should be that each of their children think, "This family would fall apart without me."

We maintain that misbehaviors such as whining would be drastically reduced if children were raised to feel this way instead of being told that they're too young, too inexperienced, or too much in the way to help out.

But how do we get there? Remember the three ways we've identified to help you decrease the number of whining incidents you experience with your children:

- Logical consequences can be used with children of any age and should be used immediately and consistently when a child whines.

- Assertive communication is a method that helps you communicate more respectfully with your children at all times. The Assertive Communication Formula is used when you want to initiate a conversation about the behaviors that are particularly troubling to you.
- Contribution is not just a technique—it is a way of life. Parents need to do more than allow their children to contribute to the family. They need to expect that children will participate in many ways.

These three methods will work together or independently of one another. Contribution is the foundation for harmonious family life. Logical consequences and assertive communication go hand-in-hand with contribution to form a solid parenting style that promotes responsibility, cooperation, and respect for others.

Let's begin by looking at the right and wrong ways to respond to whining while it is happening.

CHAPTER THREE

Logical Consequences

There are three basic ways to interact with others, including children.

The first is the autocratic model, in which someone is the "boss" and everyone else is in a position below the boss. This method of interacting uses power, manipulation, and control over others, and includes hitting and yelling as dominance techniques. There is order but no freedom.

In parenting, this autocratic model represents the "good old days" when children knew their place, didn't talk back to grown-ups, and did as they were told. This method worked well for a long time until a generation of children began to question this kind of treatment. Today, children who are raised this way generally give back as good as they get. They meet sarcasm with sarcasm, hitting with violence, verbal abuse with backtalk. In other words, these autocratic methods do not work anymore.

Permissiveness in parenting is the backlash to the autocratic method. The idea is that you should be your child's "best friend" and worry about whether your child "likes" you or not. This model brings about anarchy. There is freedom but no order. Everything goes, and some parents believe that any limit or structure thwarts their children's natural development.

However, children need structure and teaching. When they don't get guidance and firmness from parents they push harder and harder to find the limits. This leads to all types of misbehavior, some of which can be extremely self-destructive.

The model we are teaching here may be called a "democratic" approach—a middle ground between the autocratic and permissive models. This method creates freedom within order and is based in common sense. We want parents to serve as guides and teachers. You are neither the boss nor the best friend. You have a much more important role—that of teaching your children how to behave and to have empathy for others.

This model uses respectful modes of discipline and communication for the purpose of winning your children's cooperation. The most important responses to misbehavior are well-thought-out logical consequences.

From our earliest years we humans understand the concept of consequences because they occur naturally. If we touch something hot, we are burned. If, added to that, we have the verbal warning of someone older and wiser to tell us that hot things burn, we have the lesson doubly reinforced.

It seems simple, then, to suggest that using consequences, which are already part of a child's toolbox for learning, is an easy and effective way to instruct children in the behavior you want them to use.

For misbehaviors, however, parents need to intervene to teach the child how to behave in relation to others.

Whereas touching a hot stove does not necessarily require parental teaching—it is a natural learning event—ordinary misbehaviors, like whining, do require that parents respond effectively with logical consequences.

CONSEQUENCE NUMBER ONE

• **When a whining incident occurs in public, the parent removes the child from the scene.**

This action on the part of the parent is done without any comment, anger, or preaching. It can be accomplished by taking the child home or to a prearranged sitter.

The adult remains firm but kind. Once home, the parent goes about his or her business, completing the activity without the child. The child quickly learns that whining results in exclusion from events.

Parents will do best to set up a situation in which to teach their children, when they are not under pressure to actually eat the meal in the restaurant or complete the grocery shopping. This is the best time to teach your child how to behave in public. Be prepared to turn around and go home without comment once the child begins whining. You will have to practice this exercise only two or three times before your children know that you will leave a public place the moment whining begins.

In the following example, the young parents have decided their three-year-old and five-year-old need to learn how to behave in the grocery store.

• •

Sam and Karen take their two small children to the store near their house. On the way, they tell

the children they're just stopping for one or two things, and they want them to behave and not ask for other items like cookies or toys. They say, "We are going to the grocery store and we know you'll behave. We won't be buying you guys anything extra today." The expectation of "good" behavior is stated and assumed.

Once they're inside the store, however, the candy display attracts the children's attention and they ask for their favorite sweets. Mom and Dad say no, which sets off a round of whining and crying. Sam and Karen each take a child by the hand, which they had planned ahead of time, and they walk to the car. If Sam and Karen want to say anything (and, remember, no words are really necessary) they should say something like, "We see you've decided for us to leave. We can tell by your behavior. We'll try again next week."

••

The reason this consequence will work for Karen and Sam is because:

- They took action immediately.
- They didn't react with emotion.
- They used very few words and didn't overexplain or threaten.
- They had a plan and they followed through.
- They recognized the importance of setting up a structured teaching situation so they would not be under pressure or too busy or frantic to make the teaching exercise work properly.
- They expressed that there will be a next time and showed optimism that that experience will be better.

It seems simple, but few parents caught up in the whining game understand that the key to making this consequence work effectively is simply to perform the action of removing the child without displaying anger or frustration, and without justifying your behavior or lecturing the child on what he did wrong. You also always show faith that they will behave this time and the next.

Some lucky parents understand the concept because they remember situations from their own childhoods. Liz, a thirty-five-year-old identical twin, recalls the way in which her parents handled the situation when she and her sister misbehaved in public. When the family went out to dinner, for example, Liz's parents took two cars. As soon as one of the children misbehaved, an adult would simply take the child home.

At home, the parent would start to read or listen to music, totally ignoring the child's pleas to return. There

When Your Children Whine in Public
- Ignore the critical looks of those around you as you implement consequences.
- Don't let embarrassment force you to give in.
- Plan ahead and take time for teaching. Can you take two cars so one adult can leave with the whining child?
- If you must complete your errand and your child is misbehaving, simply continue on without interacting with the child. Ignore the whining completely. Do your errand quickly and leave.

was no interaction or discussion of the child's misbehavior.

Liz reports that her parents had to resort to this consequence only once or twice before the girls learned
that they would be whisked away at the first sign of
misbehavior in public.

Believe us, children who misbehave in public know
what they did without being told. You need not comment on their behavior. Giving them the time and space
to contemplate their own actions is much more effective
and respectful than verbalizing a litany of complaints.
The consequence itself speaks far more eloquently than
any words you might deliver.

CONSEQUENCE NUMBER TWO

- **In a private setting such as the home, children
  who whine should be ignored completely—not
  responded to at all.**

Here's what we mean when we use the word "ignore."
We're not just talking about verbally ignoring a child's
misbehavior. True, we're advocating that you don't engage in any conversation with your children when they
are talking to you in a whining tone. But you must also
remember that body language and facial expressions
are ways in which we communicate with our children.
Therefore, when we say "ignore," we mean that you must
also refrain from reactions such as:

- frowning
- rolling your eyes
- shrugging your shoulders
- sighing
- giving harsh looks

- using any of the other hundreds of ways in which we adults let our displeasure be known without actually verbalizing it

These nonverbal signals fuel misbehavior in the same way that lecturing and fussing do. Misbehaviors become entrenched as they continue to provide the child with a place of belonging through attention-getting power and control over others.

••

Six-year-old Seth and nine-year-old Jacob are brothers. Their mother, Kelley, allows Jacob to spend an hour Saturday afternoon riding around the neighborhood on his bicycle with his friends. The boys are helmeted, instructed as to how far away they can ride, and given a time to return home.

Seth wants to ride his bike around the neighborhood too, but Kelley says no because Seth is just learning to ride a larger bike, and she feels it wouldn't be safe for Seth to have the same freedom as Jacob right now.

Angry and upset at being left out, Seth begins to whine and wheedle, hoping he'll convince Mom to let him go. Mom doesn't look at Seth and doesn't address his whining. Instead, she leaves the kitchen area where she's been putting away groceries and goes to the backyard, where she begins to water flowers.

Seth follows her and continues his demands, his whining escalating now. Kelley goes on about her business. She waters the flowers completely, then returns to the kitchen to fix herself a snack.

At no time does she acknowledge the temper tantrum Seth is now having. Her facial expressions do not change; her body language stays relaxed as she moves from room to room doing the things she'd normally do on a Saturday afternoon at home.

Of course, Seth's high-pitched whine is annoying, his melodramatic tears are pitiful, and his claims that he's being treated badly grate on Kelley's nerves. It takes effort to remain calm and ignore a whining, crying child who's intent on following you from room to room with his demands. But Kelley knows that when Seth gets like this nothing works.

In the past, she's tried bribing him. She's rewarded him with sweets, tried to appease him by letting him have friends over, or taken him out for a special treat so that he won't feel he's being left out of the fun when his older brother goes off on an activity of his own.

The trouble is, no matter what Kelley did for Seth, she was teaching him that whining pays off. Seth was getting a lot of mileage out of his antics, and Kelley was spending much of her weekend time catering to her small tyrant. She was frazzled by his constant demands, and the whining only got worse.

Now, Kelley has made up her mind to remain serene and go about her routine, ignoring Seth's behavior. This new response to her child's whining is no more difficult than it is for her to stop what she's doing to arrange an outing for Seth or fix him a treat.

She's decided that Seth needs to learn that, as the older child, Jacob will often be doing things before Seth is allowed to. Kelley has made up her mind that Seth's whining about things must stop. She shudders to think of the teenage years she'll face if she doesn't hold firm while Seth is still young.

As Kelley continues her tasks, humming to herself as if she were alone in the house, Seth grows weary of whining and following her from room to room. He is a normal, bright child who understands that his whining isn't achieving the desired results. He knocks it off and goes to the backyard to play with his dog.

What Kelley is teaching her child is that not only will the whining fail to get him what he wants, it will not provoke any response at all. He won't be able to get her attention or demonstrate his power by making her angry or by irritating her until she gives in.

When a parent reacts to misbehavior in this way, the child quickly learns that whining as a technique is a complete bust. Hmm. Maybe he'd better find another, more effective means of communicating his wishes and desires to his parents.

But what happens when a child reacts badly to consequences? What happens when the child does something vindictive, something destructive to self or others? For example, what if Seth had retreated to his mother's bedroom and broken something she treasured? Worse yet, what if he'd taken out his anger on the family pet by kicking or striking it as he passed by instead of playing with it?

A parent who witnesses this kind of behavior may, of course, enact further consequences. However, when violence or destructive behavior of any kind occurs, parents need to take it very seriously and consider getting outside professional help.

When we tell you about setting up consequences and

teaching your children about values and proper behavior, we're talking about children whose habits may be annoying, irritating, or powerful. We're not, however, talking about children whose problems go much deeper and represent a more serious need for intervention.

You do a disservice to your whole family when you don't pay attention to serious behavioral problems or excuse them as "a phase" that a child is going through. You need to be receptive to obtaining the kind of help your child or your whole family may need if whining escalates to this destructive level.

CONSEQUENCE NUMBER THREE

- **Parents announce ahead of time that any whining done by their children will result in an automatic "no."**

This is a great opportunity to teach children about the choices they make. What you're saying is that, whereas you might have considered granting a respectful request to put off homework until a particular television program is over, any whining or disrespect brings a "no" to the request. In other words, it won't do the child any good to approach you with a whining tone. In fact, whining guarantees that whatever the child is requesting will be met with a firm "no" backed by parental follow-through.

All avenues for discussion and working out differences are closed once the child whines. The child knows the consequence because the parent has established it. You choose a time when things are calm, and you let the child know what you will do when whining occurs. You can do this anytime. Do you hold family meetings where concerns are discussed? Do you have a quiet time when you could speak to your children individually? Just choose a time when there is no friction and when you and your child can talk. Use a respectful, assertive tone and words such as:

- "When you ask me for something and you whine, I will automatically say no."
- "When you whine, I will not respond."
- "When you whine, we'll leave."
- "If you whine in the car, I'll pull over and we won't go."

Now comes the time to put your words into action. Once or twice should be enough to demonstrate that whining won't work, because it has already been rejected as an option for communicating within your family.

•••

Mom and Dad have decided to teach their daughter that her constant whining and manipulation will no longer work. They pick an appropriate time to tell her that from now on, they want her to ask respectfully for what she wants and to understand and accept the times they must tell her no. They also tell her that any whining will result in an automatic "no."

A week after her parents made this statement, ten-year-old Brittney faces a dilemma. She has previously decided she wants expensive new in-line skates. Mom and Dad have told her she can

save her allowance and pay a portion of the cost, and they'll make up the rest as her birthday gift. Brittney has saved almost half, but now her best friend is going on a special outing to a water park where they'll swim and play all day.

The parents of Brittney's friend have asked her to come along. Brittney will need to pay for entrance to the park, lunch, and anything else she wants while there. Her parents have told her she can go but she'll have to use her own money, and that means she'll dip into her savings and won't be able to pay for her share of the skates she wants.

Brittney, like any child, wants both! She begins to whine about how all the other kids' parents buy them skates and don't make them pay for anything. She acts as if having to take responsibility for her spending is cruel and unusual punishment inflicted only upon her by her mean parents.

As her whining escalates, Dad calmly goes to the phone and calls the parents of Brittney's friend. Brittney howls in protest while Dad explains that Brittney will not be going with them to the water park. Then he and Mom go about their routine, leaving the child to ponder the results of her actions.

• •

Although it was hard, Dad followed through with what he had told his daughter earlier. Instead of arguing, Dad simply took action. When Brittney escalated, Dad ignored her disrespectful behavior. One or two more times, and Brittney will get the message loud and clear: whining brings an automatic "no."

MAKING CONSEQUENCES WORK

With all three of these consequences, consistency is the key. You must use one of these three responses every time incidents of whining or misbehavior occur, and you must always follow through. How many times have you heard yourself tell your children "The next time you do that, I'm going to . . ." only to find yourself backing down when they push!

Our children become "parent-deaf" quickly, and we have taught them to be that way by blustering about what we will do instead of just doing it. Children have learned that parents don't mean what they say. We are full of idle threats, and we don't follow through. Instead, we have taught them that whining and throwing tantrums will wear us down.

But take heart! If you begin changing your patterns now to include logical consequences, and you follow through with them even though it is inconvenient for you, you will find that whining can be nipped in the bud. The changes will not occur overnight, but they will happen within a few days or weeks *if you remain consistent.*

Very powerful children will test you longer and with more intensity than other children, but these consequences will work on even the most stubborn child over time. You can bring about change if you stand firm.

It may take several times of leaving a restaurant before children realize that whining brings consequences. Eventually, however, they'll see that their manipulative techniques no longer work and that they're missing out

Remember:
- Consequences should be accomplished with a minimum of words.
- Consequences should be logically connected, not punitive.
- There is no need to remind, coax, fuss, or lecture.
- It is more important to take action than to talk. However, any words used by parents should be respectful and firm. You should talk about what *you* will do in response to whining, and then actually do it.

on meals and fun with their families when they whine and misbehave in public.

Parents feel as if they are not disciplining unless they "drive the point home" with language. We admit that it is hard to stand back and let the consequence do the teaching. But that is exactly what you need to do.

You also need to have enough confidence in what you're doing to avoid explaining yourself to your children. They are not stupid. They know why you are leaving the restaurant with them or why you are not responding to their whining.

Children, however, want to get you to explain and justify what you are doing in order to wear you down or make you so angry or frustrated that you'll give in. Don't engage in this "phony" exchange!

Many parents spend too much time explaining their disciplinary actions, because they lack confidence in the decisions they're making. Stand firm! You are doing the right thing, because you are acting with self-respect and respect for them.

Let's look at some examples.

• •

The Johnsons are sitting at a table in a family restaurant. Justin, age ten, wants to order steak, which would be okay with the parents except that it is too expensive.

When the menus arrive, the parents make it clear to their children that everyone is to order within a certain price range, and they tell Justin that he needs to pick something else, as the steak is beyond what they had planned to spend.

Justin launches into whining with statements like, "Please, please let me have it. I won't ask for dessert, I promise." When his parents shake their heads no he escalates to "You never let me have what I want. I'm not asking for that much."

• •

The parents are beginning to feel embarrassed, humiliated, and increasingly irritated with Justin's tactics.

If they were from the *autocratic school* of parenting, which includes being the boss and using punitive techniques, these parents would say something like this:

- "You're never coming out with us again."
- "You need to shut up now and if you don't, you'll pay for it when we get home."
- "How dare you cause a scene like this."
- "Act your age."

- "If I had done this to my parents they would have slapped me across the face—and I'm just about to do that to you."

Such statements are useless, and it is surprising how few parents see that this approach does not accomplish anything. These parents are issuing threats based on using their power *over* the child.

Not only that, they are being disrespectful, and the child who is whining and misbehaving knows that there will be no follow-through. Why else would he continue whining? His parents are so caught up in sounding powerful that they don't even recognize how wasted and ineffective these attempts at discipline are!

If the Johnsons were from the *permissive school* of parenting, in which parents are concerned that they are "liked" by their children, they would try to cajole Justin into good behavior. They would usually end up giving him what he wants by saying something like:

- "You can have the steak if you'll behave."
- "Honey, please don't cause a scene."
- "Oh, all right. You can have it. I'll just have to eat a salad."

Right about now you might be asking, "What is so wrong with giving him the steak?" Well, think about it. You're at a family meal where you've already asked everyone to stay within a budget. *That is a reasonable request.* You have an opportunity to teach your children about living within their means and cooperating, as well as encouraging them to think about the family as a whole.

The main reason it is so wrong to give in is that Justin

will learn nothing about thinking of others and cooperation within his own family. He isn't expected to take into
account what his parents have told him about the budget for the evening. Justin is thinking only of himself and
what he wants.

Another reason that buying him the steak is a bad response is that he gets what he wants by verbally abus-
ing his parents—and he will continue to do so in the
future. Next time, however, the item in question might
not be a simple steak. The parents are setting the stage
for an escalating series of impossible or unacceptable
demands that the child will expect to have met.

The years of arguing, miscommunication, anger, disrespect, and frustration will build and build until parents feel helpless to intervene in any effective way. *The
moment for teaching good behavior is now.* It is never too
late, no matter how old the child or how many years of
misbehavior you've indulged. Yes, it is much more difficult to implement these changes in your parenting style
after years of being either an autocrat or a doormat. It
requires even greater resolve and firmer dedication to
the principles of change that must occur if an older
child's behavior is to improve.

Parents who are truly desirous of better relationships
with their children will exercise the amount of self-
control needed to implement our recommendations,
even when the children challenge the changes that are
taking place. Hang in there. Children do respond to the
kind of respect we're advocating. It will take longer to
achieve results with older children who've built up patterns of bad behavior. Invest the time, and chart your
progress by acknowledging even small improvements in
your child's behavior. The payoff will come when you

Remember:
   If children can treat their own families abusively, think what they'll do with this power in future relationships. And how will they parent their children when the time comes to teach social responsibility and concern for others?

observe your child developing respectful relationships and empathy for others. And this will happen in time.

Parents have an obligation to think far into the future when quibbling over something seemingly minor like a steak. You should carefully consider the long-term repercussions if you choose not to teach your children how to behave.

There are several "teaching-oriented" responses that could be used to curb whining and instill within a child a sense of responsibility and empathy for others.

When Justin whines the first time about not getting the steak, both parents simply rise, politely inform the waiter they unfortunately need to leave (without calling attention to the child's behavior), and, in a calm and confident tone say to the family, "We are going to go home now. We can tell by Justin's behavior that *he's decided* it's time for us to leave. We'll try again next week."

We want to stress here the importance of these exact words, delivered in a calm and rational manner, that put the responsibility for the misbehavior and its consequences squarely on the shoulders of Justin—just exactly where it needs to be.

If the Johnsons use the wrong words and display their unhappiness over Justin's behavior, they're not getting their point across to their son. More important, they're not allowing him to see that he has, indeed, made choices by using certain behaviors. They are diluting Justin's responsibility for the situation by taking the focus off him and putting it on themselves.

If they say, "You've embarrassed the whole family and now we all have to leave because we've had enough of your acting like a spoiled brat," the emphasis has shifted dramatically. Justin is no longer the person responsible for their leaving the restaurant. Instead, the parents are the autocratic figures with all the power. It is they, not Justin, who have chosen to *make* the entire family leave the restaurant.

The fact that Justin's behavior is the root of the problem is lost as they wield their authority. Nobody, least of all Justin, learns anything by this demonstration of parental power.

It is important for parents to remember that each incidence of whining or misbehavior is an opportunity to instruct. Thinking in these terms will make it less likely

Don't Say:
- Just wait until we get home . . .
- How can you be so selfish?
- Why can't you be good like your sister?
- We're never taking you out for dinner again!
- You've ruined the evening for everybody.
- What have we done to make you treat us this badly?

for parents either to give in or to fall back on power and control.

It is extremely important that the focus remain where it should be—on the child's behavior. The child should hear in your words that *he* made the decision to misbehave, which leads directly to a consequence in which you are involved only insofar as you have to drive the car home! Let him think about that for the rest of the evening rather than feeling put upon because his parents denied him the chance to eat that steak.

The whole family could have had an enjoyable meal if Justin had respected his parents' request that he stay within their budget. His decision, and his decision alone, caused the family to miss this opportunity.

Believe us, siblings get the message too. You're teaching not just the misbehaving child but all the others as well. You must take these golden opportunities to teach your children lessons about living in a world with other people.

Your other children, or friends with whom you discuss your parenting techniques, may say that it is not fair to make everybody suffer when one child misbehaves. However, you can respond by telling them that you think there is no better way to teach children that their behaviors have an impact upon others.

The other important message is conveyed by Justin's parents when they use the correct words, "We'll try this again next week." What they're actually telling Justin is that they believe he can choose to behave in a more positive manner and that they'll give him the opportunity to rise to the occasion next week.

What a great thing! This statement shows faith in the child and basic respect for who he is and what he is capable of doing. This is the kind of encouragement chil-

> Remember:
> Again we say, if a child cannot even demonstrate respect and cooperation within the family, how will he accomplish these tasks out in the world?

dren need. Additional opportunities for the child to do the right thing are an essential part of the democratic approach.

Just stop for a moment and consider how much more effective this approach is than telling your child, "I'm never taking you to a restaurant again," an idle threat you have no intention of carrying out. We need to put an end to this kind of communication that passes for discipline in today's society.

Less effective, but still a respectful option for those of you who simply can't see yourselves standing up in a crowded restaurant and making an exit with a whining child in tow, is not to respond to his whining at all.

Talk with your spouse or your other children about anything but the misbehavior going on around you. When the waitress comes to take the order, give the child a choice between two items you can afford, and if he refuses, choose for him. All of this occurs without much talking.

It goes like this: "Justin, would you like the hamburger or the roast beef sandwich?" He grouses that he wants neither—at which point the parent says, "Bring him the hamburger." The consequence here is that he has lost his opportunity to choose for himself. This approach probably works better with a smaller child. If you start when they are small you won't have a ten-year-old acting the way Justin does!

Justin's parents could also give Justin the choice of hamburger or roast beef, and if he refuses to select one of these food items, they simply tell the server that Justin has decided not to eat. One of two things will happen if parents follow through in this scenario.

First, it is quite possible that Justin is hungry and will realize he's made an error. The child may realize he truly wants to eat dinner with the family more than he wants to put up a fuss, and he will ask (respectfully, mind you) that he be allowed to order the hamburger or roast beef after all. This is the old "second chance" ploy.

If Justin stops the whining the parents may feel pressure to give him another chance to order his food and join the family. However, this is one of those times parents must hold firm and follow through with the consequences they've enacted. To give in now and allow Justin to manipulate them is to reinforce his misbehavior. It teaches him nothing about cooperation. He learns that whining brings consequences, but that he can squirm out of them quickly.

This is why our first recommendation is to leave the restaurant. We know it is very difficult to eat in front of your child when your child has decided to misbehave in this manner.

The second thing that may happen is that Justin will continue to whine and pout, in which case the family should proceed to eat the meal they've ordered while Justin has nothing. Doing anything else is "giving in" to the whining.

Cruel? Unfeeling? Traumatic for the child? No: respectful, because the parents have allowed the child to make his own decision about whether or not he'll join the family according to the guidelines of the budget and the choices he could have made. It is also respectful because the parents did not fall for Justin's manipulation and whining. They've modeled self-respect for all the children to see because they've refused Justin's attempts to control them and the situation by acting out in public.

Justin's lesson is simple. Whining doesn't work. His misbehavior doesn't get him what he ostensibly wants—the steak. More important, Justin learns that he cannot gain negative attention and power over his parents by whining and that he must find other ways to ask for what he wants. He's also learning a valuable lesson about helping the family stay within their budget—something that's good for everyone.

Here's another example:

• •

Nine-year-old Lorie wants to watch a particular program on television, a popular prime-time teen soap opera featuring steamy situations and sexually precocious young people.

Lorie's parents feel she's too young to watch this kind of program and that the program may have a negative influence on her thinking about relationships and about becoming a teenager in general. Her parents tell her, "No, that it is not something you should be watching." Lorie begins to whine, saying that the other girls in her class get to see it.

She soon escalates into begging that if they let her watch it just this once, she'll never ask again. Next comes the slamming of doors and yelling at

her parents that they're too strict and she wishes she lived somewhere else.

••

If Lorie's parents are autocrats, they will follow her example and yell back, threatening her with all sorts of punishments—and at times dipping into revenge with statements like:

- "We wish you lived somewhere else too."
- "It would make things a lot easier around here if we didn't even have children."

This type of aggression and hurt delivered by adults is abusive and immature. When you get to this point, you need to admit to yourself that you are sinking to the child's level and are doing great damage.

Parents who are indulgent might fuss some about her attitude, but in the end they would cave in by saying:

- "If you stop whining, you can watch the show."
- "We'll let you watch it just this once."

We all know that the child won't stop whining if it gets her what she wants, and it won't be "just this once." Lorie's parents know it and she knows it too. She can always argue next week that Mom and Dad let her watch the program last week, so what's the big deal?

Respectful parenting requires thoughtful responses such as the following: Lorie's parents can ignore her whining altogether and go about their business. Whining gets no response from them. They said no and there is no further discussion.

As Lorie's demanding behavior escalates they must

stay uninvolved. Their focus must be elsewhere while Lorie whines, sulks, and slams doors.

But isn't this letting the child get away with awful behavior? The answer is no, but you need to understand why. Remember, there is a difference between ignoring your child's bad behavior because you hope it will just go away, and ignoring it because you choose to. The first is indulgence. The second is a discipline plan that *you've chosen* to implement.

In the first case, to ignore is to avoid taking action until the child drives you batty and you either explode or give in. *Making the choice* to ignore is to take a firm stand against whining by demonstrating that you will not be swayed by hysterics.

And while you're choosing to ignore the whining, think up some creative consequences as follow-through. For example, take the door-slamming part of Lorie's repertoire. A good consequence is to simply, without comment, remove the door from its hinges for a specified amount of time. Message: slammed doors disappear.

Remember that first and foremost, the child wants to get her way, which allows her unconsciously to feel important in the family. She does this by provoking a negative response from Mom or Dad. If she can accomplish this power play, she gains a mistaken feeling of significance. She is important, but for all the wrong reasons.

Lorie is creating within herself a belief that the only way she can belong is in antisocial ways. It is our job as parents to gear our responses so that the child will replace this antisocial behavior with positive and respectful methods of belonging. That is why it is so important for parents not to fall back on the anger, irritation, or retribution that reinforce the negative.

Another consequence Lorie's parents might establish

is to tell her that her whining about television will result in her not being allowed to watch it for x number of days. After a few experiences with this particular conse-quence, Lorie learns that any disagreeable conversation about the TV means it goes away—but, again, we stress the importance of giving Lorie the opportunity to do it right in the future.

Her parents should remove her television privileges for a limited and reasonable time, and tell her, "We'll see how it goes next week when the TV is back." This show of good faith and optimism in the future tells the child that parents expect changes to occur and that they be-lieve the child is capable of better behavior.

It is very important for your children to know that you expect them to make changes in their behavior and that you believe they can do so the next time the opportunity arises. You're planting the seed for positive growth when you nurture this thought.

Maintain this idea and let your children know you be-lieve in them even though they may continue to whine,

Remember:

Showing faith and optimism in your child's ability to change and grow in positive ways is the greatest gift you can give your child. We focus too much on the negative, and when children do improve we *still forcus on what they aren't doing.* Children need to know that parents believe in them and that their ef-forts, no matter how small or gradual, are acknowl-edged and appreciated.

misbehave, and refuse to cooperate. It is a powerful message of love and support that tells a child your expectations are high and that you believe they can rise to meet them. That kind of support and love are essential to encouraging positive growth in your youngsters.

With very powerful children who have become used to getting their way through whining and who will display defiant behavior when this consequence is imposed, parents may need to go so far as to remove the TV from the house.

This is an inconvenience, to be sure, but a good step to demonstrate follow-through. No explanation is required. Just take it out. No fussing or lecturing about why you are removing the television set is necessary; just proceed without comment. Trust that your child knows exactly what's going on and sees the logic in this consequence that is brought about by his actions.

Give your child the time and space to think about things and come to his own conclusions. Treat him as you would a friend—as someone who can recognize what his actions bring and who doesn't need you to try to control his behavior and punish him when he does something wrong.

That level of respect is what's required for good parenting. We're often impatient and demanding and want instant results. But human growth and development require time, thought, and consistency. As the parent, you must control your responses to misbehavior, and think before you act or speak.

Follow these four steps to implementing logical consequences:

1. Realize that whining is a problem behavior that is not good for your child.

2. Stop and think about an appropriate response.
   Don't just react.
3. Implement a logical consequence.
4. Refuse to engage in any argument or discussion
   about the consequence, by adopting a neutral
   position.

THE NEUTRAL STANCE

When your children begin to escalate after you have followed through with a consequence, you'll want to use the "neutral stance" in response.

The neutral stance is not passive. Rather, it is the result of *your active decision* not to involve yourself in your child's misbehavior. You remain calm and unwavering as your child escalates the whining in an attempt to engage you in a power struggle.

You do not let emotion guide you. Instead, you go about your routine, refusing to give in to your child's demands and offering no explanations, alternatives, or idle threats. You enact consequences and follow through without demonstrating frustration or anger and without feeling guilt.

In this way, you model responsible, adult behavior and you place the responsibility for the consequences right where it belongs—squarely on the child's shoulders. You do not muddy the waters by expressing your frustration or anger (by yelling, threatening, or giving in), because to do so takes the emphasis off the child's responsibility and puts it on you.

When parents retaliate, the child isn't reaping the rewards of his misbehavior, he's being punished by angry parents who've lost their tempers and are now exercising their own brand of tyranny. That's exactly how it looks when parents lose control and stoop to using the same behavior as their children. You can avoid this vicious cycle of escalating tempers by teaching yourself to use the neutral stance. It is simple and effective, and here's how it works.

Adopting the Neutral Stance

When you have implemented a consequence and your child escalates in order to convince you to change your mind, do the following:

- **Put a "befuddled" expression on your face.**
- **Look at the child without anger or irritation. You're confused. The child did "a" and you followed with "b." You do not understand what the problem is!**
- **Say nothing. You need not explain anything. Your child knows what happened and needs to consider the behavior and consequences on his or her own.**
- **Go about your life—make dinner, do whatever you planned to do. (Remember the example of Kelley, mother of Seth.) Say, "Oh, I've got to go read my book" and off you go.**
- **Maintain your air of neutrality. Don't seek revenge or retribution for your child's behavior. The child is experiencing the consequences of the behavior. Let it go at that.**

Don't overlook an important point as you follow these steps: you are *training yourself* to adopt new modes of parenting. Teaching yourself to react in a different and more positive manner is essential to your own growth and development. This means that you must learn to take the time to think before you act or speak in response to your child's misbehavior.

Each incidence of whining is an opportunity for teaching, not just for your children but for you as well. What a wonderful way to look at bad behavior—opportunity! And the foundation for success with each new opportunity is your increasing ability to exercise self-control. Instead of attempting to control your children, you must learn to control yourself.

The rest will follow, as we demonstrate in the following case:

•••

Janet has made meat loaf and mashed potatoes with a salad for dinner. Five-year-old Mindy sits down at the table and whines that she doesn't want what her mother has prepared and in fact is not hungry at all. She stirs the food around on her plate and continues to whimper and procrastinate about eating.

•••

If Janet were an autocratic parent she would say something like:

- "You're not leaving this table until you eat this meat loaf."
- "If you don't eat your dinner, you can't ride your bike tomorrow."
- "You better eat unless you want a spanking."
- "You go to your room right now."

An indulgent Janet would beg and cajole and try to micromanage every bite the child takes. She would say something like:

- "Please just eat something for Mommy."
- "Just have one little bite of your potatoes."
- "Now just have one tiny bite of meat loaf, please."
- "If you'll eat one bite of potatoes, I'll let you have ice cream."

As the whining ritual continues, the indulgent mom would decide to give up and fix something else for the child to eat, or go on to dessert so that Mindy would have "something in her stomach." Mom is rationalizing her child's misbehavior, as well as her own inability to stand firm.

When a child chooses not to eat the food that has been prepared, a parent has a quick and clear opportunity to use consequences and to handle the whining respectfully.

The child decides not to eat, and so the consequence is hunger. Instead of fussing or pleading when Mindy doesn't eat, Janet should finish her own meal, ignore the whining, and remove the plates, all the while talking about other things. At 9:00 P.M. when Mindy is hungry, a simple statement like "breakfast is the next meal" (respectful, assertive communication) will suffice.

Though every instinct is calling on Janet to feed her child, she shouldn't rescue or feel sorry for Mindy. The child made a decision that she needs to learn to live with. The child learns that Mother is not there to be in the child's service by cooking her something different or by rescuing her from her own decisions.

When we talk about empathy and possessing an understanding of the impact of our actions upon others, we mean just this kind of awareness. Mother is a person. Our demands upon her create extra work for her.

If, on the other hand, we eat what everyone else is eating, we're being considerate of her. Learning to think of others early and often is essential to the child's happiness in later years.

If you cannot bear for your child to go hungry, you might consider having a standard alternative, like putting the dinner the child has refused to eat in the refrigerator and offering it to her when she's hungry later in the evening.

This response is less effective than establishing the consequence of waiting for the next meal, but if you simply can't stand the thought that your child is hungry, you will at least accomplish your goal of having the child eat the meal you prepared in the first place.

Again we stress that you need not interact with your child by discussing this whole process. Simply remove the food from the refrigerator and place it before her when she indicates she's hungry. You should be polite but uninvolved in her eating, as you have other things that you must do.

Eating is a great arena for misbehavior, because parents are vulnerable in wanting their children to eat the right foods at the right times. Mealtime becomes a battleground where most children wage whining wars at one time or another. Parents are much better off if they place the food on the table and then step back and let the child decide whether or not to eat what is there.

We know that what we're proposing isn't easy. We're definitely encouraging parents to choose the more difficult path. It takes self-control and a willingness to be patient as you practice what we are recommending. You can't give in!

One father reported that he buys soda, cookies, and ice cream because he'd have no peace from his boys' whining otherwise. If he followed through with what we suggested above, he says, his children would make his life miserable after dinner. *If this isn't bribery, we don't know what is!*

And this is where you must adhere to the neutral stance—the tough step—when you must withstand the escalation of whining into anger in order for the children to see that you are not going to give in. Facing the petulant behavior and sullen faces of your children must be done with firmness, kindness, and neutrality.

However, if you cave in after a few hours of harassment you have just made a bad situation worse! Don't even start to implement our suggestions until you are sure that you are ready to see them through to the end. Consistency is the key.

Remember:

Bribery is disrespectful. It says to the child, "The only way I can get you to behave is to pay you off. You won't do the right thing without a bribe." There is nothing more debilitating to a child's self-worth than to know that a parent thinks so little of him. The expectations children hold for themselves are based largely on the expectations they perceive their parents hold for them.

You must be able to maintain your self-control and react as we've outlined for you. That's why practicing the steps and sticking to them are so important, You must model your new responses and reactions over and over until they are second nature to you. Otherwise, you're just filling up another balloon with a lot of hot air. And your children know it.

Here's a checklist of do's and don'ts for parents who want to implement consequences:

Do!

- Maintain a firm, kind, neutral attitude
- Always follow through with the consequence
- Show optimism that things will go better next time
- Let it be known that there will be a next time
- Think before you act or talk
- Make the consequence as logically related to the misbehavior as possible
- Ignore bad behavior—this, too, is a consequence
- Use consequences as soon as possible after the misbehavior occurs
- Use the neutral stance in the face of your children's escalations

Don't!

- Give in
- Fuss, preach, or lecture
- Threaten
- Bribe, cajole, remind, coax, or negotiate
- Use sarcasm
- Mimic or make fun of the child
- Explain or justify consequences
- Give second chances at the time of the misbehavior

There are exercises in chapter 6, "The Workbook," which will help you learn more about consequences. It is important to have a plan that you have thought about ahead of time so that you will know what to do. This type of responding can become just as automatic to you as yelling and giving in is now. You can see how this approach builds better relationships, but you won't realize how successful it is until you try our suggestions and see how well they work.

Start with one arena where whining typically occurs in your family and build up to changing your entire relationship with your children by tackling the problems with firm consequences and follow-through.

Children learn to whine from those around them, including their parents. How do we learn to communicate in clearer and more respectful ways? Parents talk too much in response to everyday misbehaviors such as messy rooms, not eating, whining in the grocery store— and not enough about serious transgressions.

Our next chapter will assist you in learning how to communicate in ways that encourage your children to listen. They will learn how to make requests, discuss differences of opinion, and problem-solve, instead of manipulating you to wear you down. You as the adult need to model what you want.

Remember that modeling is a stronger teaching tool than lecturing ever was!

The Right Responses to Whining

Behavior	Bad Response	Good Response
Your child whines in the store, demanding junk food that she knows she cannot have.	(Autocratic & Aggressive) You threaten and yell that you won't let her watch her favorite television program when you get home.	You and she leave the store immediately.
Your children are whining and fighting in the backseat of the car on the way to soccer practice.	(Permissive & Passive) You drive on but beg and plead with them to stop their antics. You tell them you'll buy them pizza after soccer if they'll just behave.	You pull over, turn up the radio, and start to hum along with the music. Drive again when misbehavior stops.
Your youngest child comes to you whining that his older sister won't let him play with a toy.	(Autocratic & Aggressive) You confront the sister, yelling, "Give him the toy right now. Why do you always have to cause trouble? He's just a baby."	You say, "I'm sure you can handle it." You then go on about your business and remove yourself from the conflict.

CHAPTER FOUR

Assertive Communication

Now that you've practiced the concept of responding to your children's misbehavior by establishing consequences and holding firm, your young ones have probably begun to see that you can no longer be manipulated by whining.

But the task of retraining children to communicate with you in a different way is just beginning, because replacing bad communication with no communication is not the answer. Instead, we must eliminate the problem behavior once and for all by replacing it with something that benefits both parents and children.

To completely banish whining from your children's

Remember:
It is up to you, the adult, to establish this new respectful, assertive style of communication.

repertoire of behavior, you must give them some other mode of communication to use, but it won't work if you're asking your children to do something you are not doing yourself.

Remember:
　Treat your spouse and children with the same level of respect you accord your friends and your colleagues. And keep in mind that the way you treat your spouse has a profound effect on your children.

Most of us are not fortunate enough to have been raised in a way that taught us to see and participate in truly respectful exchanges in the family unit. Family members often treat each other very badly. Things we would not consider doing or saying to complete strangers are perfectly acceptable to do and say to our spouses and children.

How do you begin to rethink your methods of communication and find a better way of interacting with your children? Let's begin by thinking about something as basic as how you speak to your family members. Here are three modes of expressing yourself that happen to correspond to the three types of interaction explained in the chapter on consequences:

- Aggressive (Autocratic)
- Passive (Permissive)
- Assertive (Democratic)

Many people think that the way to express emotions or get what they want is to be *aggressive*. They yell, demand, threaten, and are generally obnoxious and over-bearing. There are people who pretty much stay in this mode of interaction with others, and then there are those of us who resort to these aggressive tactics when our backs are against the wall.

We've all used such approaches with our misbehaving children at one time or another. If you think about those times, you will realize that your aggression either escalated the exchange or gave the child grounds to get even with you at the first opportunity.

The second type of ineffective interchange is to become *passive*. If you operate in this mode, you fail to speak up for yourself, find excuses not to take action, and generally let others, including your children, walk on you. You become the "doormat." This type of approach with your children teaches them *not* to respect you. Passive people often resort to aggressiveness when their children have pushed them to their limits.

Assertiveness is based on self-respect. You set your limits and establish how you want to be treated by others, including your children. It is also based on respect for people with whom you are interacting. Therefore, it is most important to learn how to use language assertively.

We offer two types of assertive communication. The first is simply stating what you will do and what you won't do in response to certain misbehaviors; it is usually used when establishing and carrying out consequences. There is no need to talk a lot when disciplining a child through consequences, but whatever words are used must be firm, neutral, and respectful.

The other type of assertiveness is based on a formula and is used when you want to start a serious conversation with a child (or anyone) about his behavior.

Look at the difference between these responses to a misbehaving teen:

• •

Fifteen-year-old Kristy doesn't want to baby-sit her younger sister when Mom asks her to do so because she and Dad want to go out for the evening. Kristy begins to whine and have a fit, and so Mom and Dad rush hurriedly out the door trying to avoid the conflict. Both parents are upset by what has happened and do not have a good evening.

• •

Which of these responses do you think will work best when her parents decide to discuss her behavior with Kristy?

• *Response #1—The Passive Approach:*
Mom says, "If you babysit I'll buy you that dress you wanted for the school dance." (Even though Mom and Dad have agreed that Kristy's clothing allowance has been depleted.)

• *Response #2—The Aggressive Approach:*
Dad yells, "Don't be so selfish. Your mom and I need some time away from you kids."

• *Response #3—The Passive Approach:*
Dad explains, "We're only going out for a little while, and we won't go out to dinner after the show if you don't want us to."

• *Response #4—The Aggressive Approach:*
Mom threatens, "If you act up, I'll get rid of your computer."

- ## *Response #5—The Assertive Approach:*

Mom and Dad go out, ignoring Kristy's whining. The next day, they talk to her about her behavior, letting her know how they felt and what they expect from her next time. They say, "Last night when we asked you to baby-sit for us, we felt angry that you responded the way you did. Next time we ask, we'd like your cooperation."

We hope you chose response #5 (the response based on the Assertive Communication Formula, described below), because that is the only one that will succeed in building cooperation and communication within the family. Why does it work? How? That's what this chapter is all about.

Becoming assertive in your communication will work for you and benefit the entire family. Relationships will improve. However, it takes hard work to change old aggressive or passive approaches.

First and foremost, remember your goal is twofold:

- Stop the whining by enacting consequences.
- Replace whining with an open, respectful dialogue in which parents and children speak to each other in loving and nurturing ways—even when the conversation is about unpleasant subjects.

Can it be done? You bet it can. That's what assertive communication is all about. Quite simply, assertive communication is a direct, respectful conveying of information to others about how you feel, what you think, and what values you hold. Though it may sound easy, becoming assertive is one of the most difficult skills to master.

Not only is the Assertive Communication Formula an

The Assertive Communication Formula
    "When you _____, I feel _____,
    because _____.
    What I would like is _____."

invaluable parenting tool, it also provides a method of showing our children how to be direct, open, and willing to express their feelings and wishes in respectful ways. This simple formula, based on the work of Thomas Gordon, is one we encourage you to practice. We provide examples of how this simply worded statement makes it possible to tackle the most serious subjects with your children.

Take this formula and fill in the blanks:

. . . .

"When you [<u>describe the child's action</u>], I feel [<u>describe your emotion</u>], because [<u>tell why your child's action has elicited that emotion</u>]. What I would like is [<u>describe the positive scenario you'd like to achieve and what your role or your child's role would be</u>]."

. . . .

Now, here's an example of what a parent could say after a child has whined and argued about going to bed at the appointed hour:

. . . .

"Jeremy, <u>when</u> you refuse to go to bed on time and whine about it, <u>I feel</u> frustrated, <u>because</u> I

**want you to have plenty of sleep so we don't have
a stressful morning. <u>What I would like</u> is for you
to go to bed on schedule so that you can get up
more easily."**

. . . .

All children go through stages where they test the
limits of parental supervision. And even if your children
don't openly engage in seriously destructive behaviors,
you still must teach them how to avoid such behaviors
and why these actions are not consistent with your
values.

Likewise, you may find yourself having to tackle problem issues such as bullying, using curse words, lying,
hanging out with the wrong crowd, breaking curfews, or
going to places you've told them are off-limits. You may
find yourself having to contend with children who
sneak cigarettes or alcohol.

These are all very serious, potentially inflammatory issues that you'll want to address verbally with your children (as well as using consequences), especially your
older children, and that's where the Assertive Communication Formula comes into play.

However, bear in mind that this formula is only one of
the ways in which parents practice respectful communication. Regardless of the misbehavior being addressed,
or the severity of the problem, parents should always
be respectful, calm, and firm when talking with their
children. Setting this example should begin when the
children are very young, but if you've not laid this
groundwork and your children are older, this formula
can still work for you.

When you are enacting consequences, especially when
your children are older and may be rebellious and very

vocal about you as a parent, your words are very important. They need to be kept minimal and to the point without being loud, unkind, or sarcastic. Here is the first of two examples of assertive communication:

· ·

Dad picks ten-year-old Jennifer up from school so that he can take her to the art supply store to buy a poster board for a project she must work on the next day at school.

As they drive to the art supply store, Jennifer tells Dad she wants to stop and get an ice cream cone because she's hungry. Dad says no because he's promised Mom that he'll hurry back and fix dinner so that she can get to an important meeting that evening.

Jennifer begins to whine that she's "starving," she's "going to throw up" if she doesn't get something to settle her stomach, that "Mom would stop and buy ice cream." In the past, Dad might have argued, tried to defend himself, or simply yelled at her to be quiet. This time, however, Dad wants to try something different. He uses assertive communication in this way:

"Jennifer, I can tell by your behavior that you've decided for us to go straight home." With that, Dad turns around and drives home.

Jennifer proceeds with a full-blown tantrum, screaming and crying about how much trouble she'll be in when she doesn't bring the poster board to school. Dad ignores her behavior, since he's respectfully and calmly announced the consequence of her whining.

· ·

Okay, parents. We know you're struggling with this one. Your first instinct is to make sure your children have what they need to do well in school. You are torn between teaching your children to be responsible and rescuing them from the consequences of their irresponsibility, especially when it comes to school. But how are they going to learn to take care of themselves and meet their obligations in the world if Mom and Dad leap in and take care of the problem?

And consider this: You can't teach your children these basic survival skills if you are not consistent. You can't hold the line in one instance and then cross it when it involves schoolwork. You're waffling. That's not good for anybody. You need to hold firm, and children need to face the consequences of their actions. Believe us, they will learn after one or two times that you're not there to rescue them from irresponsibility.

In our example with Jennifer, Dad is alarmed at the level of selfishness that Jennifer is beginning to exhibit, so he decides he needs to talk to her about her behavior. He doesn't want to engage in a power struggle or a shouting match, so he uses the formula to express his concerns. He waits until both he and Jennifer have had a chance to calm down and think. After dinner, Dad approaches Jennifer, who's in the den studying. Dad says:

•••

"Jennifer, <u>when</u> you whined and begged to stop when we were on our way today to get your school supplies, I <u>felt</u> disappointed and annoyed <u>because</u> you were ignoring that I was doing something for you. <u>What I want</u> is for us to cooperate

and to show appreciation to each other for the things we do to help one another.

••

Amazingly, most children respond quite well to your calm tone and sense of respect for them as people who will understand what you're saying. You're not condemning, criticizing, or threatening. You're simply providing information and asking that they try to do better in the future. The implicit message is that you also believe that your children will rise to the occasion the next time. This message is so very important to children. They must know that you expect positive behaviors from them.

It goes without saying that your words are delivered in a level, respectful, non-threatening tone. To yell out these words defeats the purpose. Remember that "assertive" is not the same thing as "aggressive." Your intent is to be understood when you speak and to convey information, and that can happen only when you present your message respectfully.

For those times when a child *does not* respond well to this approach and argues with or blames the parent for the incident, the parent simply adopts the neutral stance and quietly leaves the room. No huffing, no eye-rolling, no anger, no threats or signs of frustration are needed.

When you behave with any of these outward signs of hostility or frustration, you're simply falling back on the same behavior your child uses. The minute you begin a "tit for tat," you are encouraging the escalation of the whining into a full-blown argument that completely destroys any chance for a meaningful exchange between a parent and a child.

As a parent, you need to adopt a mature, adult way of

> Remember:
>   You teach your children respect for themselves and others when you refuse to allow yourself to be manipulated or engaged in an argument or power struggle.

handling your emotions. That's the only way you'll be able to help teach your children there are better ways of communicating than whining, arguing, yelling, or threatening. And it is the only way to curb those behaviors in your children. You can't make a child stop misbehaving by misbehaving yourself.

Realize that your children will not automatically respond with respectful words themselves. But if you maintain this type of communication over the long haul, they will eventually learn these skills. Once again, you need to be committed to the idea and continue to use assertiveness even without immediate results.

Assertive communication benefits everyone, and it does this in two ways:

- First, using assertive communication gives parents a wonderful opportunity to model the respectful kinds of communication they want their children to adopt.
- Second, assertive communication is an effective means of handling problem behaviors and stopping the escalation that we've discussed in earlier chapters.

Many of you are probably thinking that assertive communication works only with older children who understand what you are saying to them, but remember: facial expressions and body language are powerful means of nonverbal communication. Even very young children understand these kinds of cues, and they especially understand the tone of voice that's being used, regardless of whether or not every word makes sense. By working with your younger children now, you are preparing them for a time when they are older and when they will fully understand what you are saying.

However, we caution you that assuming your child is too young to understand sets up a situation where the child gets away with misbehavior for quite some time, making your parenting job much more difficult later on.

Raising children is not a process that begins when they achieve a certain age. Working with even your youngest children right from the start to establish consequences and use assertive communication can reap many benefits as the child ages and achieves a different level of emotional maturity.

We tear out our hair in frustration when we're unable to win the cooperation of our children through our misguided attempts to control them. However, we can and must educate ourselves and try new methods such as assertive communication in order to guide and train

Remember:

Assertive communication doesn't come naturally to most of us. Our aggressive or passive responses contribute to the problems we have with our children.

our children to cooperate within the family, as well as with others.

It is important to remember that the family is really the center of a broad community of interpersonal relationships and networks that we all must navigate as we go about our daily lives. Do not think that your children don't already know this. From the moment they leave home for day care or school or even to play with neighborhood children, they enact the behaviors that they've learned within the family.

That's why learning better and more effective ways of communicating within the family also gives everyone powerful tools to use in all areas of life. You'll find all the practices that we're describing in this book surprisingly helpful in your adult relationships, whatever the environment.

Now, here's a second example of assertive communication. You'll see immediately how the formula can and should be implemented by taking a look at a typical scene that most parents have experienced at one time or another:

. . . .

It is Saturday morning and Jody, who is thirteen, has promised to meet her friends at the mall. Jody's mother, Carol, has told her that she won't be able to go until she completes her chores and cleans her room.

Jody begins to wheedle and whine, arguing that none of her friends has to do chores before going to the mall. She begs her mother to let her go, promising that she will do her chores later in the day.

At first, Carol, a working mom who is hard pressed to take care of all the domestic chores herself, tries to ignore Jody's behavior by moving to the laundry room and beginning her own weekend work.

However, Jody follows her there and escalates until she is demanding that her mother let her go to the mall because "it's not fair" to make her delay her pleasurable activities and keep her from seeing her friends. "Why do I have to do everything around here?" she pouts, her petulance finally pushing Carol's buttons.

"Sure, Jody, you do it all," she says sarcastically. "I guess I don't do anything."

Carol's sarcasm fuels Jody's whining, which has the opposite effect from what Carol would like. The escalation of the argument leaves Carol feeling exhausted and inept at parenting her own child. She reasons that it is easier to do Jody's chores herself than to listen to the incessant whining and complaining.

"Okay, Jody, go ahead," she says wearily as she shrugs her shoulders and gives up the fight.

Jody goes off to the mall without a backward glance at her mother. Carol gives up her plans for an afternoon outing of her own so that she can do the extra work she's taken on by giving in to Jody's demands.

• •

Jody has learned that whining and manipulation are effective tools of communication, and Carol feels like a wimp because she is once again stuck with all the chores. She knows in her heart that she's sending Jody the wrong message about responsibility, respect, and cooperation.

If Carol had more self-respect and a stronger sense of her leadership role as a parent, she would not give in to Jody's whining and misbehavior. She certainly wouldn't do the child's chores for her.

Let's say that instead of giving in, Carol counters Jody's whining by going on about her business, moving from room to room doing her own chores and ignoring Jody. The child's frustration and anger escalate until she is having a tantrum and slamming doors. Mom refuses to waver. She continues to ignore the bad behavior. At some point, Jody will simply run out of steam. Her antics aren't achieving the desired effect, and she'll stop.

Now it is time for Carol to use the Assertive Communication Formula. As the parent, Carol needs to address Jody's rude behavior, but she needs to pick a time when things are not heated between them. The following morning, Carol might say something like:

• •

"Jody, <u>when</u> you make a statement like you did yesterday about your doing everything around here and me not being fair, <u>I feel</u> irritated, <u>because</u> you are negating what the rest of us do to keep the house running. <u>What I'd like</u> is for you to speak to me more respectfully."

• •

Or she might say:

"Jody, **when** you said what you did yesterday about you doing everything around here and me being unfair, **I felt** angry, **because** I think you were trying to make me feel guilty and start a fight in order to make me back down. **What I'd like** is for you to be more considerate when you talk about these things and take responsibility for your chores."

• •

Either one of these responses would be effective. Carol shouldn't say any more because nothing more needs to be said. As a parent, she has modeled, and therefore taught, the type of communication she wants for her family. She has rationally and respectfully informed Jody how she feels about her actions.

Carol has also extended a great gift to her daughter. She's opened the door to a new, respectful way for the two of them to relate to each other. Now that she's seen how it is done, Jody may want to continue the discussion in a respectful manner herself. If she takes that step and responds to her mother in the right way, all the better. A lot can be accomplished if the two are able to talk about how to make things better between them, and their relationship will improve.

Is there a child who actually enjoys the alienation and misery that whining and fighting with his parents bring? We don't think so. Parents who show their children better ways to express themselves are teaching life skills that will flourish and enhance their children's relationships with others for the rest of their lives.

If Carol continues to interact with Jody in this way, calmly and without resorting to the same kinds of sulking, whining, and angry blowups that her daughter uses, Jody will eventually get the message. It is only by observing her mother's new approach over time that Jody will learn to appreciate and emulate it. Parents must remember that we are our children's models of what behavior and language should be and that our consistent use of techniques of assertiveness is what shapes our children's behavior. There is no simpler way to say it.

Our children, no matter how they might protest this idea, *do want to be like us.* We are their points of reference, the first adults whom they interact with, idealize, and try to imitate. Because of this, what we do and say in response to what's going on around us matters much more than we may think.

We are showing our children, no matter how young they may be, how to operate in the world. That is quite a responsibility and one that many parents have not fully considered. Role models do exist in our culture, but never forget that you are the first and most important one that your children will encounter.

We need to truly appreciate the impact our behaviors have on our children, especially our teenagers. Teens are adept at making their parents feel that, at this "advanced" stage of development, they are very nearly

Remember:

Maturity is our greatest asset, something our children do not yet have. Let's share that gift with them as we establish respectful behavior and expression within the family.

adults themselves and therefore beyond parental influence. The truth of the matter is that the teen years are fraught with anxiety and a multitude of difficult decisions. Our teens desperately want and need guidance at this juncture in their lives.

Never forget that the way in which members of a family speak to one another is of the utmost importance, because destructive verbal attacks can be as debilitating to children as abusive physical behavior.

Note the tone of the two responses Carol might use. The statements are informational. Carol does not criticize or ridicule her daughter, or otherwise undermine her. Rather, she calmly communicates her own feelings and perceptions matter-of-factly, without using emotionally charged language that does nothing more than escalate the conflict.

Don't Say:

- You're so spoiled and ungrateful!
- How could I have raised a child like you?
- I'm sick of you and your complaining.
- Why can't you be good like your cousin?
- Go on. You never do anything anyway.
- Shut up or I'm putting you on restriction.
- If you cared about this family, you wouldn't be acting like this.
- You're so selfish you can't think of anyone but yourself.

Think about it. When someone begins to criticize us, we all have a tendency to turn off *what* they're saying and tune in to *how* they're saying it. In other words, we miss the message completely because we're no longer listening. Instead, we may become defensive and angry, responding with heated words that cause hurt feelings and an escalation of conflict with little hope of resolution.

There are no two ways about it: you are learning to do things differently, just as you are asking your children to learn new ways of communicating with you. It will be unlikely that your children will change the ways in which they react and respond unless you do the same.

It is essential that you be the one to stop the escalation of whining or arguing. You must teach yourself to walk away from the conflict and give yourself the valuable time both you and your child need to cool down. When you take the emotion out of the discussion and focus on what exactly you want to say and how you can best convey the message, you're more likely to be heard and understood. And you *must* be heard and understood if you are going to be an effective teacher who wishes to communicate values, priorities, and responsibilities to your children, even under the most difficult circumstances.

In the best possible scenario, your use of the Assertive Communication Formula will generate open, respectful dialogue between you and your children. You may be pleasantly surprised to see that your calm approach and lack of emotion actually whet your children's desire to have a reasonable conversation with you. Most of us know from our experiences with our closest friends that honest, heartfelt communication works. Why wouldn't this also be true for your children?

By sharing your needs and concerns, you are letting your children know that you are receptive to allowing them to do the same, as long as there is no hostility,

Remember:

You don't want to make your child feel bad or guilty or unloved just so that you can win the argument. That's why it is important to think about what you want to communicate and choose an appropriate time to do so—after the emotions have calmed. What you really want to do is convey something important about yourself in a way that is both respectful of the child and self-respecting as well. Your children want to know who you are and what you think about important issues. Don't deprive them of this experience by yelling or saying hurtful things because you're frustrated or angry.

anger, or manipulation. Your children may look upon your new approach as an opportunity to talk openly with you about the things that matter most to them. The assertive approach establishes a fundamental atmosphere of trust, something that may have been missing from your relationship with your children up to this point.

However, if your children meet your attempts to communicate this new way with a rebuttal, merely maintain your pleasant demeanor, say nothing, and get on with your life. In this way, you're refusing to acknowledge or "feed" the misbehavior in your children.

You are trying, instead, to create an environment that will lead to good discussion and greater understanding of the power of our words and how using them carelessly can affect others. You want your child to

> *Remember:*
>
> Assertive communication instructs on many levels because it is about the appropriate demonstration of personal power, which is the ability to speak up about what's important to you with respect for yourself and the person you are talking to. It tells your children, *"I respect and love you, and I want you to understand me and my feelings because you're important to me."*

learn to do the right things, but anger and conflict are not teaching methods that work. Modeling a new way of communicating with respect and caring is the answer.

As more and more parents are learning, it is very difficult to exert a positive influence on our children by dominating, commanding, ridiculing them, or giving in. The only real influence we have with our children is found in the strength of our relationships with them. One of the ways we establish good relationships is to give up our need to control or "make" the other person *be* a certain way. Rather our responsibility is to control our own responses to the behavior of others. If you think about it realistically, that is the only true power we have. Manage yourself—not your children. It is this realization that can lead to an open, loving, respectful relationship where each person feels valued, respected, and important.

A healthy side benefit of assertive communication is that children learn how to express their feelings and desires without whining. Instead, children begin to see that there are much more effective modes of communication to be found in behaviors that are positive and much more likely to obtain the responses they're really after.

Assertiveness doesn't guarantee that children will always get what they want, but it does create an atmosphere in which what they say is appreciated, respected, and listened to, and we maintain that these things are always more important to children than just getting what they want.

Added to that, the relationship skills your children build within the family are skills that will benefit every other relationship they enter into. Respectful, assertive communication is the foundation of any lasting relationship. How many failed marriages today would have benefited from the trust and respect that assertive communication builds within a partnership? And there is no better place to learn these values and practice these skills than within the family.

Assertive communication also allows us and our children to appropriately express and communicate feelings of anger. We're not about to tell you that the guidelines we're providing will work some kind of magic so that you and your children will never be angry with each other again. Feelings of anger are as much a part of living as feelings of love or compassion or caring.

Remember:
In the long run, teaching your children to communicate respectfully with others is more satisfying *to the children* than getting their way through whining.

The danger of these angry feelings is that they can become destructive when they are fueled by the emotionally charged language and behavior that we've come to accept. We say, "I really lost it," or "I blew my top," or "I was out of control" to describe what happens to us when we become angry without being able to properly channel those feelings.

Assertive communication helps us to take a deep breath, phrase our language constructively by using the "When you say or do that, I feel this" formula. Parents know that when we act on anger, we're modeling behavior that tells children it is okay to demonstrate anger without regard for the feelings of others.

Worst of all, children learn poor habits that they'll later fall back on in an attempt to get their own needs met. Never forget that the bottom line of all this discussion is that children—and adults—whine because they want something, and the whining is the tool they've identified as the one that will get them what they want. It is learned behavior; it doesn't simply appear out of nowhere.

With assertive communication, we're *talking* about our anger rather than *acting on it* by succumbing to the strong emotions that anger provokes within us. Inappropriate expressions of anger are often verbally or physically abusive, damaging the self-esteem of others and creating a hostile atmosphere. These are the last things most parents want to do to their children.

Assertive communication lets us talk about the fact that we *feel* angry *without demonstrating it.* Anger won't go away by itself, but it can be diffused and examined by this process. And it is getting increasingly important that we teach children to handle their feelings of anger in appropriate ways.

Children who've never learned to express anger in healthy ways can become terribly destructive and aggressive teenagers and adults who cause great harm to others.

Our next example illustrates how explosive a situation between a teen and his parents can become:

• •

Mike is a young man of thirteen. His parents, after some consideration, have decided that he is too young to attend a late-night rock concert with a new group of friends they have not yet met.

Mike is hurt and angry, accusing his parents of "not trusting" him and treating him "like a baby." He is at an age where he desperately wants to grow up and do all the exciting and wonderful things he thinks older kids experience.

Mike's mother and father are understandably worried about his entry to the teen years and all the changes and negative situations he will face as he grows into adulthood. They don't want to hold him back, but they do want him to take on responsibility in a slower, more gradual way.

His parents have said no, and now Mike becomes petulant and whines, something he's always done even as a young child. In the past, he's been able to wheedle what he wants out of them by incessant whining and nagging that have played into their feelings of guilt and their secret fears that they're not as good at parenting as they should be.

Mike whines that they let his sister go to a slumber party when she was younger than he is,

and he implies that if they don't think he's trust-worthy then maybe he'll be driven to do some-thing wrong. "Why can't I go with my friends," he whines. "Why not?"

Dad has had enough. He's never been able to stand Mike's whining, and his own inability to deal with it has made him frustrated and angry at himself. He feels that if he were a better father, Mike wouldn't act this way. His self-doubt rapidly turns into anger, and he responds by yelling, "You can't go because we say so, and that's it!"

Mike turns sullen, muttering just loud enough for his parents to hear, that he's sick of being treated like a baby while his older sister is al-lowed to do whatever she wants.

Mom sees Dad's temper kicking in and just wants to reestablish peace. She knows that Mike and his dad can get into some pretty loud argu-ments once things begin to escalate, and she also knows that the whole family feels the impact of these battles when they're not resolved.

She tries to reason with Mike, explaining that his sister's slumber party was a far different situ-ation. His sister had been at the home of a girl who'd been her friend for many years. In addi-tion, the other girl's parents had been there to supervise the slumber party activities, and the two sets of parents knew each other well.

However, her explanation falls on deaf ears. Mike doesn't want to hear or consider that his case is very different from his sister's or that his parents might have a valid point.

Torn between wanting Mike to stay home and wanting to stop the escalating conflict between her husband and son, Mom sinks back into her familiar pattern, which consists of being the indulgent one who wants to keep everybody happy.

Just as Dad has done, Mom begins to doubt herself as a parent. Maybe Mike is right. Maybe she doesn't want her little boy to grow up and so she tries to keep him at home and keep him from doing the things all the other boys his age are doing.

In the back of her mind, Mom wonders if by trying to set limits now she's actually setting the family up for an all-out war when Mike is older, say sixteen or seventeen, and his whining becomes even more difficult to deal with. She begins to feel her resolve crumble.

Sensing Dad's growing anger does little to help. Mom knows there's going to be a shouting match if she doesn't do something.

Mike senses victory. He has orchestrated scenes like this one before. He's not a bad kid, but he definitely knows what he wants and how to get it. He continues chipping away through whining and manipulation, thinking only of himself and the rock concert he wants so badly to attend.

Mom is on the verge of saying, "Okay, you can go, but only if you promise to behave and get home early."

• •

Either way, through provoking Dad's anger or getting Mom to back down, Mike wins. He'll get his way and blithely go off to attend the rock concert, seemingly oblivious to the turmoil his behavior has created within the family, or he'll engage his parents in a power struggle that upsets the whole family and demonstrates his dominance.

Mike hasn't developed a level of empathy that would make him care that his selfishness and manipulation have a very serious effect on his parents. He won't be there to see the argument they have later, nor will he be there to experience the tension that his behavior has caused or the worry his parents endure as they wait for him to return home.

This is a scenario fraught with anxiety, disappointment, and fear. It is certain to be repeated over the next few years unless Mike's parents find a way to deal with his misbehavior and begin to assert themselves confidently as parents and guardians who must teach as well as nurture.

Displays of anger and bouts of indulgence fuel misbehavior. In Mike's case, the pattern dates back to his early childhood and has continued up to what will soon be a crisis point.

Ideally, Mike's parents should have nipped this behavior in the bud when Mike was much younger. Consequences could have been established long ago so that Mike would have known by age thirteen that whining or complaining would bring an automatic "no" that no hysterics on his part could alter. Mike's parents could have shown him early on that his misbehavior was not a tool that would bring any discussion, compromise, or progress on the issue at hand.

If his parents had been more assertive, Mike would have learned long before the advent of his teen years that there is a much more effective and loving way to communicate. He'd have learned that there is an appropriate means of beginning a discussion, asking for things directly, and raising his objections.

> *Remember:*
> It is very important for children to learn, as early as possible, that they may not always like our decisions, but they can, in the context of loving, respectful relationships, accept them.

He'd also have learned to accept what his parents deemed appropriate, listening carefully to their side of things and trusting that they have his best interests at heart.

The truth is that Mike's parents haven't established the patterns that promote and maintain the behavior they'd like Mike to exhibit. Is it too late? Not at all. Just because we haven't set the consequences and assertive communication models in place doesn't mean that we can't begin immediately to repair past mistakes and to create a more cooperative spirit for the future.

Let's consider how the scene might play out if Mike's parents understood and practiced the use of consequences and assertiveness in dealing with their son's whining and manipulation.

• •

Mike approaches his parents and asks to attend a rock concert with his friends. His father says no, calmly explaining, "Mike, we know you're disappointed, but your mother and I don't feel comfortable letting you attend the concert. We'd like to meet your new friends before we give you permission to stay out late at night with them."

It is important to note here that Dad does some initial explaining (which we've indicated parents need not do when enacting consequences), because Mike's original request was made without whining or complaining—he simply asked if he could go to the concert. Dad said no, but he wanted Mike to understand why he was making this decision. It is only later, when the whining and misbehavior begin, that Dad stops talking and ignores Mike's behavior.

Mike's parents feel he is too young to attend the rock concert with a new set of friends they've not yet had a chance to meet and get to know. They may sometimes have doubts about their parenting choices, but by and large, they know they are the adults in the home and that they love their children and want what's best for them.

They're willing to take on the decision-making role and see it through because they know their children need guidance, patience, and love as they develop into responsible young adults.

● ●

Mike begins whining and complaining, trying to manipulate and control the situation by making his parents feel angry, guilty, and frustrated. Mike begins to accuse his parents of treating him like a baby and allowing his sister to do things they won't let him do.

The parents go on watching their program on TV. They ignore Mike as he continues to whine. Finally, Mike gives up and goes to his room. His parents remain unruffled, but they know that nobody's happy with the way things ended. They want to change the way they and Mike interact.

The next day, Dad speaks to Mike and addresses his son's misbehavior by using assertive communication, saying, "Mike, <u>when you</u> became angry and abusive because we would not let you to go to the concert, <u>I felt</u> angry <u>because</u> it seemed that you were trying to wear us down and make us change our minds. I thought you didn't care about how we felt. <u>What I'd like</u> is for you to treat us with more respect. Your Mom and I love you and want a better relationship with you than that."

That's all Dad says, and he only says it once. He simply states his case and refuses to engage in an argument about the original decision or their reasons for making it. His tone is pleasant and informational, and then he lets it go.

Mom and Dad are both committed to creating a new parent-child dynamic with their son. They are modeling respectful, honest behavior with the intent that Mike will learn means of communication that are more effective. They're also demonstrating that they'll no longer allow him to drive a wedge between them and get his way with whining.

Mike won't get this new dynamic overnight, but if his parents are consistent, Mike will begin to understand and imitate them as he learns new communication skills. Things will improve for everyone.

Parents need to trust in their relationships with their children and assume that better behavior will ensue as a result of taking a firm stand, using consequences, following through, and by talking with their children assertively when important things need to be discussed.

Children experiment with different behaviors in order to find their place in the family. They will use negative behaviors such as power, attention getting, and revenge as long as these techniques serve to bring them the significance they want. When a child is provoking a parent to anger, he is feeling a tremendous sense of power in being able to push the right buttons to get such a strong response from adults.

So how can children learn other ways of belonging? What can we as adults do to help them with this task? Read on!

CHAPTER FIVE

Contribution

In earlier days in American society, when our economy was largely agricultural, people functioned at the basic level of "If you don't work, you don't eat." This point of view extended to all members of the family, including children.

While we've moved beyond raising our own food into a more complex and materialistic culture, we've forgotten the one essential good that comes from living off the land—the sense of belonging that comes to those who pull their weight, have responsibilities, and make a contribution to their families and to their society.

In many contemporary homes, children are asked to do nothing at all to contribute to the maintenance of the family. In some homes, children are expected to do no more than clean up their rooms and pick up their toys, if that. Even these two very minor requests are usually met with resistance.

If it is such a major effort to get children to do one or two things in their own rooms, you may wonder what it must take to get them to assume more responsibility. Parents don't even want to think about the giant task of battling it out with their children to get things done. They'd rather just give up and do it themselves or, more likely, shut the door to the children's rooms and hope no new disease develops as germs accumulate.

But think back to those earlier times. It was a given that the individual learned his value by participating and contributing within the group. Why have we let this wholesome practice die? It is more difficult in our present day because we no longer "live off the land," but the feeling that we can contribute is no less essential to our mental and emotional well-being.

If you think back to when your children were toddlers, you'll probably remember their overwhelming enthusiasm for everything they saw you doing. They wanted to help mop, do the laundry, cook, make beds—whatever they saw others doing became a goal unto itself. They always wanted to learn how to do things and help out.

Where did all that enthusiasm go? Why now can't you get the very same children to voluntarily lift a finger to help around the house? This natural learning process

Remember:

Our children need to learn to belong by experiencing the results of contribution in their first group, the family. Why in the world would we want to raise children to expect that their parents will do everything for them? What kind of adults will they be if they never learn to help out and think of others?

is usually stopped cold by parents who want things done "the right way" (perfectly and quickly) or who are too busy to take the time to teach a child who wants to help.

What we forget is that a child who wants to help is really a child who wants to learn. We stop them from learning the good things, like how to participate and contribute to the running of the household, and discourage them from belonging in this positive way.

Parents today are often too tired, in too much of a hurry, or more concerned that the task get done "correctly." Early on when a preschooler wants to wash the dishes and the parent says, "No, let me do that— you're too little," that parent has taken the first step toward discouraging the child's natural desire to contribute.

When the child is fourteen and won't get off the sofa to help you bring in the bags of groceries from the car, you wonder why his attitude is so bad. Well, welcome to the end result of not allowing your child to help.

Nobody disputes the fact that our lives today are busy. When we brush off our child's attempts to contribute, it is usually because we are concerned about the wasted time involved in letting the child "play" at doing chores. It takes too much time for a child to do the dishes. Besides, something might get broken or the dishes won't be clean enough. We'd rather jump in, get it done, and get it over with. On top of that, we're usually way too concerned about perfectionism. We know the child isn't going to do a great job, so we simply won't allow the child to try.

If this is your attitude, you are missing wonderful opportunities to allow your children a place in the family through contribution every time you shuffle them off to watch television while you do the chores yourself. If you don't teach your children now, while they're at their most eager and enthusiastic stage, you'll be facing a much tougher time later after they've adopted power and revenge as ways to belong and feel important.

Let the preschooler wash the dishes. You can wash them again later, after he has gone to bed. If you close off positive avenues of contributing to the family, your child will quickly discover that importance is achieved in this family by negative attention-getting devices and power struggles.

A sense of belonging and significance within the family unit is as essential to human beings as the air we breathe. We all need to feel that we have a place of importance there. If positive routes are closed off, children will discover negative ones instead. Let's take a look at a mother who has learned that her responses as a parent can make a huge difference in the way her daughter finds a positive place.

• •

Kathy has been trying to get her seven-year-old daughter, Cindy, to set the table for the last several months. She has bribed Cindy, and reminded her over and over that this is her job.

At times Kathy has even gotten angry at Cindy when she would start to set the table, then dawdle and finally wander off without completing the job. Kathy would give up in the interest of getting dinner on the table and set it herself, but she'd let Cindy know how irritated and angry she was. The child typically just shrugged her shoulders and went back to watching her television program.

One day a new opportunity presented itself. Little Cindy came into the bathroom around 5:00 P.M. where Kathy was bathing the two younger boys. She asked her mother if she could make the fruit salad for dinner that night.

Kathy's first impulse was to say no, but, having been exposed to the ideas we are trying to teach in this book, she instead told Cindy, "Sure, go ahead and make the fruit salad." When Kathy went to the kitchen sometime later, she found that Cindy had broken the fruit into small pieces, mixed in yogurt, and then added chocolate syrup. Cindy had also set the table!

The chocolate–fruit salad concoction wasn't the most appetizing-looking dish Kathy had ever seen, but she forced herself to taste it. To her surprise, it was good. Dad also later tried it.

Both parents noted Cindy's efforts and thanked her for her help, exclaiming how good her salad was. Cindy beamed and, at last report, was still setting the table regularly without being reminded. Her attitude has improved in other areas as well. Her sense of contribution to the family is heightened because Kathy showed faith by backing off and letting her try.

• •

If Kathy had said no to Cindy's offer to help, she would have been sending a multitude of negative messages, including:

- You can't do it.
- I can do it better.
- I don't trust you to be able to handle it.

These messages that come from the simple "no" of a tired, overtaxed, or impatient parent can have serious repercussions for children. Let your children help *in any way that they're able*, regardless of how imperfect or slow their contribution may be. Tell them that their efforts are appreciated and expected within the family.

However, one thing we stress is not to go on and on about a child's contribution. Children need to know you appreciate their efforts, but they sense when you're just trying to make them feel good with false sentiments. A simple statement or two noticing what the child has done to lighten your load will do wonders:

- "Thank you for helping me fold the laundry."
- "You really worked hard to help Dad wash the car. It looks great."
- "I was so tired after work. When you set the table without me having to ask you, I was really grateful."
- "You must be proud of yourself for the good job you did on the dishes."

It is not necessary to say anything that's not true. Had the fruit salad been inedible, the parents could have tasted it and thanked Cindy for her willingness to help or set the table and let it go at that.

We hope you can see that in addition to providing a sense of responsibility and gaining skills in doing tasks, a focus on contribution promotes social feeling and empathy for others. A child who is helping to prepare dinner begins to develop an appreciation of what others do for her. She starts to understand the give-and-take of social living.

Here's an example of what can happen when families

indulge their children rather than allowing or expecting them to contribute and have feelings for others.

• •

Donna had a bad case of the flu and wanted nothing more than to sleep. Eight-year-old Megan had grown used to their nightly ritual of reading together just before bed. She became irate when Donna said that they couldn't read together that night because she was sick.

Megan whined and cajoled, which made Donna feel even more drained and exhausted. Finally, Megan threw a first-class tantrum, crying and acting as though her world was going to end.

Because Donna was so sick, she did not give in, which would have been her normal response after fussing at Megan. In fact, Donna was so tired that she had no energy to react to Megan and simply ignored her whining. The child finally wore herself out with her screaming and crying and fell asleep on the floor next to her mother's bed.

As sick as she was, Donna still recognized that something significant had occurred. Megan's temper tantrum had ended all by itself. Ignoring the misbehavior of the child had worked. Megan was asleep, and Donna hadn't had to drag herself out of her sickbed and read to her child to pacify her.

• •

How should we expect our children to behave when circumstances like these occur? What we want is for them to understand and to pitch in, to think of others' needs. We want them to help rather than insisting on having their own way. They need to look on Mom's problem as their own and rally to help her.

They will have learned, if you have taught them, that acting responsibly and having empathy for others is what is expected. Parents would have modeled and used logical consequences to teach them that it is their job to pitch in with household tasks and all the other things that keep the family unit running smoothly, and most especially when a member of the family is ill or needs help.

Of course, as with anything, the earlier you begin teaching your children to be responsible, the fewer problems you have later on. Winning your child's cooperation and teaching about contribution can be done in several ways, some of which we've already discussed but would like to reiterate here.

- Use logical consequences when tasks are not completed.
- Ask a child to help and, if you get a negative response, back off with a show of optimism for the next time you ask.
- Have the children participate in deciding which tasks will be done by whom.
- Let the children help decide what consequences are logical for tasks they don't complete.
- Don't make it your job to remind children what their assigned tasks are or when they should be done.

Logical consequences that are useful when teaching your children what happens when the chores are not done include:

CHORES	CONSEQUENCES
Failure to do dishes or take out the garbage	Mom does not prepare dinner because she can't cook in a messy kitchen.
Failure to set the table	No food is put out for dinner. Mom simply puts the food she's cooked away for tomorrow night's meal.
Failure to place dirty clothes in the hamper	The only clothes washed are those in hamper. The child's clothes remain dirty.
Failure to clean up room	Parents take garbage bags into the room by an agreed-upon deadline and fill them with all the toys, clothes, etc. that are out of place. The bags are removed for a predetermined amount of time.
Failure to vacuum	Dad vacuums and pays himself with money out of the child's allowance.

It is essential for parents to follow through when establishing consequences such as these when they are teaching their children about contribution. It is also im-

> ### Sometimes the Best Thing That Can Happen in a Family Is for Mom to Break Her Leg!
>
> When Mom simply can't do all the things she normally does, the children in the family have to assume more responsibility. It has been our experience, however, that most children welcome these opportunities to contribute and do so willingly.

portant to focus on the positive by acknowledging the changes that occur when the child begins making an effort to do things.

Some tips to help you be consistent are:

- Once you've announced the consequence, stick to it. In other words, if you've said you can't cook because the garbage hasn't been taken out, then *don't cook.* Don't respond when your children rush and remove the garbage. Second chances are not given.
- As badly as you want to, avoid reminding your children that if they don't get their chores done a consequence will occur. This is disrespectful on your part. Merely set up the consequence, follow through with it, and say no more.
- Follow through with the consequences every time. Be kind and firm, but don't waver from your purpose—which is to teach children through logical consequences that their lack of responsibility has its effects.
- Don't argue with children or justify the consequences. Trust that children are not stupid. They know what they've done. Just enact the

consequence and get on with whatever you were doing.

- When children argue and whine, don't give in. Remain neutral, kind, and maybe just a little confused by the children's retaliation, which seems to come from an apparent inability to recognize that their misbehavior has brought on these consequences.
- Always show faith that things will turn out differently next time. Say, "We'll see how next time goes . . ." and leave it at that. Your message to your child becomes one of optimism with the reassurance that there will be another opportunity to do things differently. Also, implied within this show of faith is that you expect that the child will do right the next time.

Here's how it works:

• •

You ask your thirteen-year-old son to help bring in the groceries that are out in the car. He will probably grumble and whine, perhaps say "No" or "In a minute—when this program is over."

You can try the usual responses like ordering, complaining, yelling—*all of which are expected by this child.* Or instead, you can do something unexpected, saying, for instance, "Well, maybe next week . . ." and you bring the groceries in yourself. Let it go at that.

Many times, children will jump up and pitch in, stunned by the lack of negative response from you. Next, instead of lavishing praise on the child for doing something that by all rights he *should*

have done anyway, you simply say "Thanks" and leave it at that.

• •

This approach is very difficult for parents, because they're so used to getting caught up in power struggles with their children that they don't stop to think that the groceries are not the issue at all. Power is the issue.

Now let's think about a structure you can use to delegate chores and begin raising expectations for your children's participation and contribution within the family. Set aside a time each week when you and your children sit down together and discuss which chores must be done and who is to do them.

A fair way to divide household chores is the time-honored practice of drawing straws. The one with the longest straw gets to select the first chore, and then you move around the circle, letting everyone select a chore until everything is assigned.

Mom and Dad are equal participants with the children. Next week the chores are rotated. That way, everyone gets a chance eventually to be responsible for every chore and nobody feels "put upon."

When someone fails to do a chore, consequences

Remember:

If you simply refuse to play the power game and diffuse the struggle with a calm and hopeful response, the avenue of cooperation is opened. Children are more likely to respond in a positive way.

such as the ones we've suggested above ensue. To take this a step further, a good thing for parents to do is ask the children to help set up which consequences should follow which neglected chores. You'll find your children will come up with innovative and logical consequences.

Making family decisions and laying out ground rules should involve everybody. That's what contribution is all about. Don't forget that teaching children about contribution should begin as early as possible.

Give consideration for the level of tasks you're assigning smaller children, so that they're able to accomplish them to some degree. They might not be able to carry out the trash by themselves, for example, but they will be able to help Mom or an older sibling do it, or they can be in charge of sorting items for recycling, or be responsible for putting in the garbage can liners. The same principle applies to doing dishes, folding clothes, or any other chore.

We often have parents who ask us about tying their children's allowance to the chores they're supposed to do. We believe allowances should never be based on doing those tasks that keep the family going. It is, at its base, disrespectful to pay children to do what they ought to be doing in the first place. The message the child hears is "My parents believe I won't do anything to help out unless I'm paid. I must be bribed to do the right thing." How low an opinion is that?

Children should receive allowances so they can learn how to handle money, what things cost, how to save, and how to use money to benefit others as well as themselves. But their help within the family is needed, expected, and appreciated. A "subsidized contribution" provides no sense of belonging.

It is often very effective to use a child's allowance as a *consequence,* however. We don't mean withholding a child's allowance as a "punishment" for not doing chores. Rather, we're talking about a much more logical approach that we'll demonstrate by going back to our friend Carol and her daughter Jody, both of whom we met in our last chapter.

As you will recall, Jody wanted to bypass doing her chores to go to the mall to meet her friends. Our past example showed you how Jody wore her mother down until Carol gave in and did the chores herself. This time, however, Carol responds in a different way.

The confrontation between mother and daughter plays out exactly the same way as it did in the previous chapter, and Jody goes off to the mall without lifting a finger to complete one of her chores. This time, however, Mom refuses to respond to Jody's whining.

Carol simply ignores the child's behavior, not saying yes or no when Jody demands to be allowed to meet her friends.

Statements such as the ones Jody has made about her unfair burden and having to "do everything" merit no discussion, because both mother and child know the statements are patently untrue and are designed to manipulate. Worse yet, Jody's tone is disrespectful and inconsiderate.

Taking her mother's silence as a sign that it is okay to go, Jody leaves. Carol will still end up doing Jody's chores, but she will use the consequences method to let Jody learn about the repercussions of her behavior.

On Sunday when Jody receives her allowance, Carol withholds a portion to pay herself for doing Jody's chores. When Jody questions why she is getting less money, Carol states in an even tone, "I ended up doing your jobs when you went to the mall, and so I am paying myself to do your work out of your allowance."

Remember when we told you not to tie a child's allowance to the completion of chores? Well, we're not contradicting ourselves here. Jody's allowance is given to her whether or not she does her chores. The fact that she went to the mall instead of completing her tasks does not mean she receives no allowance. But when Jody leaves the house knowing Mom will finish the chores for her, she has, in essence, "hired" her mother to do the things that must be done in her absence. Mom is simply taking that payment out of Jody's allowance.

If she wanted to, Carol could instead prepare a bill and present it to her daughter at the same time that she gives the child her allowance, telling Jody to pay for maid service. Do you see how this method of enacting consequences is a very different transaction from paying a child to do her chores? In one instance, a child is being rewarded for doing work that should be part of her normal contribution to the family. To pay a child for contribution is disrespectful, because you are saying, "I can't get you to do the right thing without paying you." Ultimately, this undercuts a child's ability to belong to the family in a positive, loving way.

In the second instance, the parent is establishing a consequence that teaches the child that her failure to contribute means someone else must do more. That person who takes on the extra burden deserves compensation. In the same vein, we're not opposed to paying children to do extra things that are asked of them above and beyond what you've all agreed is regular household maintenance.

Once again, remember that a minimum of talking and absolutely no punishment or hostile confrontation is needed. All that is needed is a simple, respectful, calmly stated sentence such as: "I had to do the dishes for you Wednesday night, so I deducted two dollars from your weekly ten-dollar allowance to pay myself."

Mom has her own chores. When she has to take on extra duties because of Jody's negligence, she should be compensated.

That's it! Walk away and let the child digest that bit of information. If you do your part to present the consequences calmly in this manner, you will see changes in your child's behavior.

Contribution is the antidote for all types of behavioral problems. When kids can belong positively, they will. Nothing is more important for a parent to realize than this key concept: you must allow your children the opportunity to contribute.

You may have a cleaning person who takes care of your home and a lawn service, but you must still grocery shop, care for pets, entertain, share meals, take out the garbage, water the yard, and do countless other things each day to make your home a safe and comfortable place. All of these household chores provide opportunities for children to contribute.

There are, however, many other ways besides household chores to carry the idea of contribution forward with your children. Consider these:

- You may belong to a church or civic organization that is involved in community service projects. Let your children share this involvement when it is appropriate.
- Perhaps you're helping with a food drive for the needy or a project within your neighborhood. Involve your child.

- If you're planning a family trip, let your children take responsibility for some part of the packing or organization of the event.
- Don't forget the extended family. Let your child take responsibility for an elderly relative who would welcome a visit. Encourage your children to write cards and letters to relatives who live at a distance. Don't forget the art of "thank you" notes.
- When you attend a family dinner or reunion, your children can help host or entertain others through an activity such as a musical recital or a display of new skills learned in dance class.
- Older children can read to the younger ones or help them orchestrate games or events so that a family function runs more smoothly.
- When your children have birthday parties, encourage them to invite children in their classes who are usually left out, not just the ones who are popular.
- Consider enrolling your child in a scouting program. These organizations offer excellent outlets for contribution, as they are community-service oriented.
- Let your children take charge of recycling efforts.
- Give your children the responsibility of clipping and sorting coupons from the Sunday paper.
- Have your children set out the breakfast dishes and pick the morning cereal for the family.
- Children can groom and walk the family pet.
- Let them be responsible for turning off the lights, TV, or stereo before everyone leaves the house.

These are only a few of the ways you can encourage contribution. Ask your children to help you come up

Remember:

There are abundant opportunities for children to learn about making their own special contributions. A child's self-esteem and positive self-image can come from participating in even the smallest of these efforts.

with more ideas. You might be surprised at some of the great things your little ones will suggest when you engage them in a brainstorming session to determine what things they can all do to help out. Start by using the four most important words a parent can say: "I need your help."

Imagine what will happen when you encourage more and more of these kinds of behaviors. Every time a child does something for someone else, it is a contribution to the welfare of the family or society in general and should be applauded as such. You need to be very conscious of giving your children the satisfaction that contribution brings, regardless of how old they are or how perfectly they do their chores. Show appreciation for effort, teach them how to do tasks without fussing at them, and avoid reminding or giving in.

Children respond beautifully when they feel they are needed, that their help is essential, and that we really count on them. Don't allow fatigue or perfectionism to stand in the way of letting your children function as productive members of your family.

Everything you do to encourage your children to belong in positive ways combats whining and other misbehaviors. When children can belong in a positive way, there is no need for them to act negatively.

Now turn to the next chapter and start applying the ideas and methods we have taught you in this book.

Remember:
Every child should think, "This family would fall apart without me!"

CHAPTER SIX

The Workbook

In this chapter you will find a workbook filled with exercises, diary pages, and self-tests to help you chart your progress as you work to teach your children respect, cooperation, and contribution. We suggest that you use the workbook as you begin to try new responses to your children's whining and misbehavior. You may wish to set aside some time every evening to go over the events of the day and record the behavior you and your children exhibited.

It is not enough to think differently about how to respond to your children. You must practice new behaviors so that they become as automatic to you as your old behaviors of yelling or giving in. The workbook helps you "practice" your responses by recording them at the end of the day, noting where you fell short and where you succeeded.

Use our exercises to generate your own. Be creative and find things you and your children can do together to solidify new behaviors and attitudes.

SAMPLE 14-DAY PARENT PROGRESS DIARY

Day 1:_____Friday, April 30_____
(date)
Today my child(ren) and I experienced these incidents of whining/misbehavior:

Joey whined because he thought Suzy got a larger scoop of ice cream after dinner than the scoop I served him. He made such a fuss demanding more ice cream and telling me that I always gave Suzy more that I wondered if I did show favoritism to her because she's still just a toddler.

When my child(ren) misbehaved, I used the following responses and techniques:

I knew that he was just pushing my buttons like he always does, but I still had some doubts. I thought maybe I should just give him another scoop of ice cream to get him to calm down. Then I remembered that that's not the right way to train him to do things differently. So I did what I'd read about and just ignored his behavior. After the kids went to bed I re-read the chapter on consequences and saw that I could also have taken his bowl of ice cream away and just said nothing. Next time I'll try that.

The end result was:

Joey kept whining for a few minutes, but I just left the room to go sort some laundry. I noticed he did quit complaining, and when I went back to the family room, he'd eaten his ice cream.

14-DAY PARENT PROGRESS DIARY

DAY 1: _____
                    (date)

Today my child(ren) and I experienced these incidents of whining/misbehavior:

When my child(ren) misbehaved, I used the following responses and techniques:

The end result was:

14-DAY PARENT PROGRESS DIARY

DAY 2: _____
(date)

Today my child(ren) and I experienced these incidents of whining/misbehavior:

When my child(ren) misbehaved, I used the following responses and techniques:

The end result was:

14-DAY PARENT PROGRESS DIARY

DAY 3: _____

(date)

Today my child(ren) and I experienced these incidents of whining/misbehavior:

When my child(ren) misbehaved, I used the following responses and techniques:

The end result was:

14-DAY PARENT PROGRESS DIARY

DAY 4: _____
 (date)

Today my child(ren) and I experienced these incidents of whining/misbehavior:

When my child(ren) misbehaved, I used the following responses and techniques:

The end result was:

14-DAY PARENT PROGRESS DIARY

DAY 5: _____
                    (date)

Today my child(ren) and I experienced these incidents of whining/misbehavior:

When my child(ren) misbehaved, I used the following responses and techniques:

The end result was:

14-DAY PARENT PROGRESS DIARY

DAY 6: _____
(date)

Today my child(ren) and I experienced these incidents of whining/misbehavior:

When my child(ren) misbehaved, I used the following responses and techniques:

The end result was:

14-DAY PARENT PROGRESS DIARY

DAY 7: _____
(date)

Today my child(ren) and I experienced these incidents of whining/misbehavior:

When my child(ren) misbehaved, I used the following responses and techniques:

The end result was:

14-DAY PARENT PROGRESS DIARY

DAY 8: _____
(date)

Today my child(ren) and I experienced these incidents of whining/misbehavior:

When my child(ren) misbehaved, I used the following responses and techniques:

The end result was:

14-DAY PARENT PROGRESS DIARY

DAY 9: _____
(date)

Today my child(ren) and I experienced these incidents of whining/misbehavior:

When my child(ren) misbehaved, I used the following responses and techniques:

The end result was:

14-DAY PARENT PROGRESS DIARY

DAY 10: _____
(date)

Today my child(ren) and I experienced these incidents
of whining/misbehavior:

When my child(ren) misbehaved, I used the following
responses and techniques:

The end result was:

14-DAY PARENT PROGRESS DIARY

DAY 11: _____
(date)

Today my child(ren) and I experienced these incidents of whining/misbehavior:

When my child(ren) misbehaved, I used the following responses and techniques:

The end result was:

14-DAY PARENT PROGRESS DIARY

DAY 12: _____
(date)

Today my child(ren) and I experienced these incidents of whining/misbehavior:

When my child(ren) misbehaved, I used the following responses and techniques:

The end result was:

14-DAY PARENT PROGRESS DIARY

DAY 13: _____
                    (date)

Today my child(ren) and I experienced these incidents of whining/misbehavior:

When my child(ren) misbehaved, I used the following responses and techniques:

The end result was:

14-DAY PARENT PROGRESS DIARY

DAY 14: _____
(date)

Today my child(ren) and I experienced these incidents of whining/misbehavior:

When my child(ren) misbehaved, I used the following responses and techniques:

The end result was:

PHRASES TO MEMORIZE

It is not a bad idea to commit the following key phrases to memory. How we say things is very important. But don't take these words and use them punitively—you will defeat the whole purpose.

1. I see that you have decided that we should go. I can tell by your behavior.
2. When you _____, I feel _____, because _____. What I would like is _____.
3. I love you. I don't like what you are doing.
4. Thanks for your help.
5. I need your help.
6. We'll try this again tomorrow/next week.
7. When you whine, I'm not going to respond.
8. I can tell you put a lot of effort into _____.
9. What do you think should happen the next time you _____?
10. You must be proud of yourself when you _____.

RESPONSE OR REACTION? PARENT SELF-TEST

Take this test, then turn to page 148 to see our answers.

1. It is way past his bedtime, but five-year-old Johnny is not tucked in and sound asleep. He's dawdling and whining, refusing to put on his pajamas and demanding a snack and more television.

    His mother is working late, and it is Dad who must take the parental reins. What things might Dad do?

2. The spring dance is one week away, and Mom has promised her thirteen-year-old daughter, Jessica, a

special dress and told her how much she's willing to spend. They are shopping at the mall when Jessica spies the dress of her dreams.

The only hitch is that the dress is twice as much as Mom wants to spend. Mom asks Jessica to continue looking around for another dress, but Jessica begins begging and whining to buy the expensive dress. She snatches it off the rack and goes to try it on despite her mother's protests. It fits like a dream, and Jessica continues insisting it is the only dress for her. Salespeople are beginning to look their way, and Mom is embarrassed for both of them.

What's this mom to do?

3. It is nightmare alley in the grocery aisles. Mom and Dad are doing the weekly shopping with their two children in tow. The kids have already caused problems by running down the aisles and getting in the way of other shoppers. Now they begin pulling products off the shelves and whining to get Mom and Dad to buy them.

When they come to the aisle that holds children's toys and games, the misbehavior gets even worse. Mom's threats of punishment haven't worked, and Dad finally tells the children they can each pick out a toy if they'll promise to behave themselves until the shopping expedition is over.

Peace reigns for a few blessed moments, but pandemonium begins again as the children whine for ice cream on the way out of the door. What did Mom and Dad do wrong?

4. Dad has told his sixteen-year-old son, Mark, that he could borrow the family car for a Saturday night date.

However, when Mark's report card arrives and his grades are poor, Dad tells him he's on restriction and can't use the car.

Mark whines about the unfair grading at his school and the humiliation he'll undergo when he tells his date he has to cancel. He escalates and begins yelling about how terrible things are for him at home. Dad explodes and tells Mark that if he's so unhappy he's free to leave and try to make it on his own. What happened between this parent and child that could have been avoided?

RESPONSE OR REACTION?
PARENT SELF-TEST ANSWERS

1. Instead of reminding and nagging Johnny to put on his pajamas and go to bed, Dad should simply ignore the child completely. It is past the child's bedtime, and Johnny knows where he's supposed to be. The child is a "ghost" that Dad neither sees nor hears.

   When the child whines, complains, or cries, Dad must turn off the TV and go about his business, tuning the child out and removing himself from the scene. For example, Dad could go to bed himself and read, or go to the bathroom with a book and shut the door. The child will eventually grow tired and go to sleep whether or not he is wearing his pajamas or has brushed his teeth.

   Remember, Johnny's goal is to demonstrate power by getting Dad angry or frustrated. When he does not succeed, he eventually gives up the whining and is less likely to try it again.

2. Frankly, the time to leave the mall was the minute Jessica began to pester and whine to have Mom buy a dress that is too expensive. Mom should simply have said, "I see you're not ready to buy a dress right now because you're not looking within our price range. Let's go home and try again in a couple of days."

   Then Mom needs to turn and walk out of the dress department and out of the mall, ignoring all the whining and complaining that may follow as she and the child return home.

3. Threatening children with punishment "when we get home" is verbal hot air. Parents rarely follow through, and kids know it. Also, Dad's caving in and letting them each pick out a toy is just as ineffective. Now that the boys have achieved their aim—to get Mom and Dad to buy them something—the toys are of no significance.

   Next they whine for ice cream and try to assert their power there. Placating children just encourages them to use whining again. Instead, since both parents are shopping, one parent should simply have taken the offending child or children out of the store while the other continued shopping for groceries.

   When Mom takes the children back to the car she should say, "We're leaving because your behavior tells us that you've decided to go. Dad will finish the shopping by himself." Again, we stress that the time to take action is right away, the moment the misbehavior begins, not when you and other shoppers have been tortured through half the store.

4. Dad's angry outburst doesn't do a thing for this situation. Instead of putting Mark on restriction, Dad

should have stated that since his grades are poor, Mark needs to spend the time studying instead of going on a date. Therefore, Dad is unwilling to let Mark use the car.

Dad should have walked away from the argument, ignoring the whining and escalation and continuing on with whatever he was doing. Children have some deep-seated fears, and one of them is expulsion from the family unit. We should never threaten our children with being cut off from us. We're their parents no matter how they behave.

Dad missed a golden opportunity to let his child know that he loves him but that he would follow through with consequences when Mark's grades are bad. Dad should follow up by saying something like, "Son, when you whined and got angry after I told you to cancel your date, I felt irritated and hurt by what you said because I was concerned about your grades. I would like us to speak with each other more respectfully. I'll try to do my part to make that happen in the future."

JUST BETWEEN YOU AND ME

An Exercise for Parent and Child

Prepare some individual homemade flash cards that read,

"When you _____,"
"I felt _____," "because _____."
"What I'd like is _____."

The day after an incident of whining and escalation, when things have settled down a bit, ask your child to sit with you and do this flash card exercise. Let your child hold the cards up first and you give the responses. Now hold the cards up for your child and let him give his responses about the incident. Then you can talk about the differences in the ways you both saw the incident and how the two of you can solve the problem in the future.

For example, Mom says, "Billy, let's talk about what happened in the grocery store yesterday."

Billy holds up the flashcards, and Mom says, "When you ran around the store grabbing things off the shelves and whining when I told you to put them back, I felt embarrassed because you were acting out of control and we were bothering other shoppers. What I'd like is for you to help me in the store and not cause a disturbance."

Next, Mother holds up the cards for Billy, and he says, "When you didn't buy me ice cream, I felt angry because I wanted it. What I'd like is to have something from the store for me, too."

Using this exercise can now lead into a problem-solving discussion and a plan that the two of you can agree on in order to avoid future scenes in the store. This exercise promotes respect and cooperation because you're taking the child's point of view into account and are allowing him to take part in solving the problem.

MIRROR, MIRROR

An Assertive Communication Exercise for Parent and Child

For this exercise you will need a large handheld mirror, some blank sheets of paper, and pencils.

Find a quiet time when things between you and your child are relatively calm. Have a specific behavior in mind that you'd like to address (an incidence of whining or misbehavior that you've ignored and now need to talk about).

Tell your child specifically what topic you wish to address (e.g., "Janey, we need to talk about what happened last Thursday when I asked you to complete your homework before you watched television, and you started whining").

Ask your child to take a blank piece of paper and write down what she thought you should have done in response to her whining, and why.

Tell your child you will also take a blank piece of paper and write down what you'd have liked your child to do in place of whining, and why.

Then exchange the papers. Take the mirror and tell your child that now you're going to read her paper to the "mom" who is in the mirror. Look at your image in the mirror and address it as if you were the child. Cover all the points your child puts on his or her sheet of paper. Be polite, respectful, and caring as you speak to the mirror.

Ask your child to do the same—take the mirror and address the "Child" as if she were the mother, reading from your piece of paper and adopting the same polite, respectful tone you've used.

Then tell your child that in the future you want communication between the two of you to be based on respect and empathy, even when you disagree. Ask your child to stop and remember what it felt like to look in the mirror and imagine that he or she is the parent addressing the child.

Tell your child you will do the same as long as the conversation does not degenerate into whining and arguing. You will listen and respond with respect and empathy.

Here's an example of what we're talking about:

Janey writes, "I think Mother should let me watch television when I want."

Mother writes, "Janey, school is more important than watching television. After you finish your homework, you can watch television."

Mother reads into the mirror what Janey has written, but in a non-whining, calm and respectful tone.

Janey reads into the mirror what Mom has written, assuming the role of the parent and adopting the same tone Mother has modeled.

After you complete this exercise, discuss the tone and the respectful communication that you wish to share with your child even when you disagree and even when she is making unreasonable requests or statements. Talk about how you will practice using this tone and this approach with each other from now on.

This exercise is effective because it gives parent and child a chance to observe their words being read by the other person. This develops empathy and also enhances listening skills.

RESOURCES

Alberti, Robert, and Michael Emmons. *Your Perfect Right: A Guide to Assertive Behavior.* San Luis Obispo, Calif.: Impact, 1995.

Bower, Sharon, and Gordon H. Bower. *Asserting Yourself: A Practical Guide for Positive Change.* Reading, Mass.: Persus Books, 1991.

Dinkmeyer, Don Sr.; Gary D. McKay; and Don Dinkmeyer, Jr. *The Parent's Handbook: Systematic Training for Effective Parenting.* Circle Pines, Minn.: American Guidance Service, Reprint, 1997.

————. *Raising a Responsible Child: How to Prepare Your Child for Today's Complex World.* New York: Simon and Schuster, 1973. Revised edition, New York: Fireside (Simon & Schuster), 1996.

Dreikurs, Rudolph. *The Challenge of Parenthood.* Reprint, New York: Plume, 1992.

Dreikurs, Rudolph, and Loren Grey. *A New Approach to Discipline: Logical Consequences.* New York: Penguin, 1993.

Dreikurs, Rudolph, and Vickie Stolz. *Children: The Challenge.* New York: Dutton, 1964. Reprint, New York: Plume, 1991.

Gordon, Thomas. *Parent Effectiveness Training.* New York: Peter H. Wyden, 1970.

Lott, Lynn, and H. Stephen Glenn. *Positive Discipline A–Z: 1001 Solutions to Everyday Parenting Problems.* Edited by Jane Nelson. Rocklin, Calif.: Prima, 1993.

McKay, Matthew; Martha Davis; and Patrick Flanning. *Messages: The Communication Skills Book.* Oakland, Calif.: New Harbinger, 1995.

Smith, Manuel J. *When I Say No, I Feel Guilty.* New York: Bantam, 1986.

Swets, Paul W. *The Art of Talking So That People Will Listen.* New York: Fireside (Simon & Schuster), 1983.

INDEX